Celebrity Needlepoint

Celebrity Needlepoint

by JOAN SCOBEY *and* LEE PARR McGRATH

The Dial Press   New York   1972

ACKNOWLEDGMENTS

The efforts of many people have gone into this book, not least, of course, the delightful people you will meet in these pages. We would also like to thank others whose contributions are less visible: Clarice Adee; Dorothy Bagnall; Julian Bercovici; Roy Blakeman; Judy Crichton; Shirley Fields; Deborah Harding; Beebe Kline; Mildred Lanier, Curator of Textiles, Colonial Williamsburg Foundation; Monica Meenan; Susan Meyer; Augustine Pennetto; Susan Ochs; Liz Scofield; Grace Shaw; Helen Smith; Betty South; James Traub; Kelly Wallace and Helen Bolotin, The Needlecraft Shop, Sherman Oaks, California; Warren Wallerstein; and Jane Wilson.

Library of Congress Cataloging in Publication Data

Scobey, Joan.
  Celebrity Needlepoint.

  1. Canvas embroidery. I. McGrath, Lee Parr, joint author. II. Title.
TT778.C3S35   746.4'4   72–3085

Printed in the United States of America
Book Design by Lynn Braswell

First Printing

PHOTOGRAPHS IN COLOR BY GEORGE JANOFF

COORDINATION BY ANNE KNAUERHASE

Contents

Illustrations

Celebrity Needlepoint

Introduction

"What do the simple folk do?" sang Arthur and Guinevere in *Camelot,* as they wondered about the private pastimes of their subjects.

A more intriguing question through the ages has always been: How do the celebrated—the famous whose public lives exist in a glare of scrutiny—amuse themselves when their time is their own?

One answer is—they needlepoint.

Catherine of Aragon stitched Tudor roses and thistles on cushions for her husband Henry VIII, who had a great interest in embroidery. Mary Queen of Scots whiled away years of confinement in English prisons stitching intricate canvases, sometimes as gifts for her ruling cousin, Queen Elizabeth, sometimes working joint projects with a jailer, always signing her needlepoint regally and pathetically with a crown. Elizabeth shared her interest in needlework, one of the few enthusiasms they had in common, and insisted that her ladies-in-waiting learn the art of stitchery. If they did careless work, she sometimes flew into a royal rage, ripping it out for them to do over.

Needlepoint continued to be a diversion of the leisured aristocracy. William and Mary of Orange covered almost every bench and chair in their castle with needlepoint, for Mary wanted to be the "patron saint" of English needlewomen. Two hundred years later, English queens were still stitching. Dowager Queen Mary of England spent the last nine years of her life needlepointing a splendid floral rug that was eventually auctioned for $100,000, the proceeds going to charity.

Today, the famous still needlepoint, but leisure seems to have disappeared. Perhaps because time is so precious to them, the busy people interviewed for this book waste very little of it. Indeed, the more pressing their commitments, the more productive these celebrated people seem to become. And the pleasure that they have found in adding needlepoint as a further creative dimension to their lives is one that we all can share.

Joan Scobey
Lee Parr McGrath

Claire Bloom

"LOVE" proclaims Claire Bloom's favorite needlepoint, simply and boldly. The message is stitched in large brown letters on a beige field, completely filling the fourteen-inch square pillow. "I love the simplicity of the design," says the petite English actress and, one presumes, the message as well.

The spare contemporary design of the pillow is adapted from a signed lithograph by the well-known artist Robert Indiana, which hangs in her daughter Anna's room. "Its colors are so bright—reds and oranges—and I didn't think they'd be good for a needlepoint pillow," Miss Bloom says, explaining the change of colors. "And I wanted to match the beige and brown bedroom." The finished pillow, backed in brown suede, rests in the bedroom of the elegant New York town house she shares with her husband, Hillard Elkins, producer of *Oh! Calcutta!*

Mr. Elkins is the recipient of another piece of his wife's needlepoint, a pair of slippers in a tiger pattern, also in brown and beige. "They're the colors that go best in our bedroom, explains Miss Bloom, "and they're the colors that he likes for his feet," she adds fondly. Although brown and beige would seem to be favorite colors, Miss Bloom shakes her head vigorously. "No, no. I really love flowers, but I think you can have just enough of them to a point. And I had done a lot of pillows and cushions."

Miss Bloom started to needlepoint on the set of an early film, finding, as many screen actresses do, that the waits between scenes seemed interminable. "It can be so boring, and run on for hours and hours. You'd go crazy." That first project was a fruit design and, with over fifteen films to her credit, including *Limelight, Charly, Look Back in Anger*, and *The Spy Who Came in from the Cold*, there has been ample opportunity for her to stitch a variety of floral pillows as well. The LOVE pillow was produced on the London set of *The Severed Head*.

While Miss Bloom has found needlepoint a productive way to pass the time on a film set, she does not take it to her theater dressing room, feeling that a stage play requires continuous concentration. With recent roles in a pair of Ibsen plays— *Hedda Gabler* and *A Doll's House*—and the historical drama *Vivat! Vivat Regina!* she has not been able to work on any needlepoint currently. But she does have her next project at hand, a "mat," which, she explains in her lovely British voice, "is simply not large enough to call a rug."

Favorite needlepoint: LOVE pillow, fourteen inches square

Design: Adapted from a Robert Indiana lithograph, in brown and beige

Canvas: No. 10 mono

Stitch: Continental

Claire Bloom stitched this striking design, based on a Robert Indiana lithograph, in beige and brown to match her bedroom.

Rocky Cooper Converse and Maria Cooper Janis

Maria Janis with a floral rug of her own design: sunflowers beneath a white lattice.

To several generations of moviegoers, Gary Cooper was the epitome of the homespun, laconic frontiersman. In private life, however, his cosmopolitan interests included a sophisticated taste in art shared with his wife and daughter, who translated their own love for paintings into another visual medium—needlepoint.

The favorite needlepoint projects of this mother-daughter team of stitchers are a pair of Gauguins originally made as pillows for their Beverly Hills house, but which now hang in Rocky Converse's summer home in Southampton. "When I came East," she says, "I had them unstuffed and framed. They were much too good to be pillows." Maria Cooper Janis recalls working companionably on the two Gauguins. "Mother and I began to needlepoint when television started. We used to work on it together in the evenings watching TV. After eyeglass cases and the usual things, we did two Matisses. They're simpler with their flatter colors. Then we graduated ourselves to Gauguin."

Mrs. Converse chose the two Gauguin prints from her art library and took them to a needlepoint shop to be painted on canvas. After finishing the Gauguins, she had a Van Gogh landscape transferred to canvas, and she and Maria have passed it back and forth without finishing it for almost ten years. A particular fondness for Picasso is reflected in Rocky's New York City apartment by paintings, a number of bright tabletop sketches dedicated to her, and a photograph of Picasso in conversation with Gary, Maria, and herself, taken when the family spent a summer in southern France visiting Picasso. But she has not yet attempted to capture him with needle and yarn. "I think Gauguin, Picasso, and Matisse are all especially suitable for transfer into needlepoint," she comments, however.

Maria, now married to the renowned pianist Byron Janis, is achieving recognition for her own paintings, and has reached the stage of designing original needlepoint canvases. "I use acrylic when painting the canvas, thinning it to work like watercolors," she says. Her needlepoint is unusual for the subtle blending of colors, which she frequently uses in a somewhat pointillistic manner, sometimes stitching with different shades of yarn in the needle at the same time. "I don't find it difficult,"

Detail from "Women With White Horse," a Gauguin painting faithfully reproduced in needlepoint by Rocky Cooper Converse. The entire reproduction is shown in full color in the insert following page 22.

Detail from another Gauguin, "Horses on a Pink Beach," this one stitched by Mrs. Converse's daughter Maria Janis. The entire reproduction can be seen in the insert following page 22.

she says. "I just find it a lot of fun. I'm so used to mixing paint —and this is just mixing threads. It's much slower than painting, though," she admits wryly.

One of Maria's own drawings, transferred to canvas and stitched into a pillow, is a portrait of the Château de Thoiry outside Paris, one of the great houses of France. It was there that her husband recognized the lost manuscripts of two waltzes in Chopin's own hand. The Count who owned the château had long been a great admirer of Byron Janis, and, when the pianist was playing in France, asked him to examine the manuscripts that had been discovered in a vitrine. "Of course, Byron knew their importance immediately," Maria recalls with a trace of remembered excitement in her voice. "Later there was a beautiful concert at the château—just a short program, but of course the waltzes were the highlight." Working from photographs, her own sketches, and memory, she outlined the château on canvas, then worked freely, blending colors into an enchanting fairy-tale castle set in a grand park.

Both mother and daugher tend to work when traveling. Mrs. Converse, now the wife of prominent plastic surgeon John Converse, often stitches when driving with her husband

11

between her New York City apartment and her Southampton summer home. "I needlepoint in the car," she remarks, "so I don't have to look at the Long Island Expressway."

Maria, who accompanies her husband around the world as he concertizes, finished the château pillow while returning from the inauguration of the Kennedy Center in Washington, D.C. "I was determined to get it done," she remembers. "I was in a race, stitching automatically in the dark as the car went through the tunnel to Manhattan."

Even though mother and daughter are less frequently able to sit together with their needlepoint these days, the mutual interest is still a shared one. Maria's newest project is a sunny floral rug for her house in France, and she describes the origin of its design. "Mother had a big arrangement of sunflowers in the country that she copied from a Van Gogh, and I copied it from her."

Favorite needlepoint: "Women With White Horse" and "Horses on a Pink Beach"

Design: Adapted from the Gaugin paintings by Mazaltov, Inc., New York

Canvas: No. 14 mono

Stitches: "Women With White Horse" by Mrs. Converse in continental; "Horses on a Pink Beach" by Mrs. Janis in basket-weave

Kathryn Crosby

"Learning is living, and living is fun," says Kathryn Crosby, describing her energetic approach to life. Certainly nothing but real enjoyment could explain her vast array of accomplishments since marrying Bing Crosby. She has added singing and dancing to an acting career, written a book, earned her cap as a registered nurse, collected and excavated pre-Columbian pottery, studied Spanish, French, and German, and earned degrees in both elementary and secondary education, which enables her to teach her own three children when the family is out of the country and to substitute in local public schools when they're at home. Obviously needing something to do in her spare time, she has recently discovered a new enthusiasm— needlepoint.

Never one to aim small, Kathryn tackled an ambitious project immediately, working out an original needlepoint design large enough to cover a coffee table. "It is a line drawing that I traced on graph paper from a Miguel Covarrubias illus-

13

Kathryn Crosby translates her interest in primitive art into needlepoint by designing a table top with black-and-white African figures.

Detail from Kathryn Crosby's table top.

Kathryn Crosby displays her partially completed canvas.

tration in an early book on Africa," she explains. "I loved the purity of design and the fact that it dealt with Africa, where Bing has made six safaris now. Each time I look at it, I'm back in the high grasslands of Tanzania, kneeling like the figure, waiting for the sun to set. Incidentally, none of the little men in the design looks like his neighbors, but each has his own personality. I'm even thinking of giving them names," she says. The needlework was planned as a Christmas gift for Bing —a project of approximately six months—and now tops a custom-made Parsons table in the Africa room at the Crosbys' ranch.

In producing it, Kathryn plied her needle in a variety of settings. "I have worked at ladies' luncheons, which keeps me from talking too much," she recounts with amusement. "I've stitched while jetting from one end of the country to the other with my sister Frances, who has started some needlepoint of her own. And I've done it in Baja California waiting for the fog to lift so we could go scuba diving. I'm also unhampered when the children are doing their schoolwork and I must monitor them. It allows me to nod, encourage, correct, and still achieve something on my own." Best of all, Kathryn has discovered that stitchery is the perfect accompaniment to marriage with a sports fanatic. "With needlepoint in hand, I can last through four football games on TV in a row," she says triumphantly, "even if there is also a baseball game being broadcast on the radio."

Learning as she went along on her ambitious project, Kathryn worked on a double-weave canvas, which allowed her to use gros point for some areas, then to split the canvas to capture fine details in petit point elsewhere. "I used basketweave for the background and large solid areas, changing to continental when I filled in the little men with petit point." The only time she ran into trouble was when she neglected to count spaces, with the result that her first row was four stitches longer than her second. She quickly learned that any geometric or regular design, and all borders, must be counted—useful information since needlepoint will be a continuing part of Kathryn Crosby's busy life and one that she plans to link with her other interests. "Of course, my main reason for the needlepoint is to capture some of the magnificent pre-Columbian designs we have found in shards in Mexico," she says. "I love working these mammoth jigsaw puzzles, and I hope, even if we can't get complete items, we can reproduce the design on needlepoint for fun and posterity."

Favorite needlepoint: Tabletop with African figures, approximately twenty-four by twenty inches

Design: By Mrs. Crosby from a Miguel Covarrubias drawing, in black and white

Canvas: No. 10 penelope

Stitches: Basketweave and continental

Ann B. Davis

Whether you know her as Alice, as she's called by "The Brady Bunch," or Schultzy from the old "Bob Cummings Show," off camera the quickest way to identify Ann B. Davis is by the piece of needlepoint in her hand. "I carry it with me everywhere—like my purse," she says exuberantly. "I never go out of the house without it because I just might be kept waiting for five minutes, and I think, oh boy, that's free time to do my needlepoint!"

A good part of her "free time" occurs on the set of "The Brady Bunch," where, in fact, Ann first became interested in needlepoint. "When you're doing television or film work, you spend a great deal of time sitting around, and you can't really concentrate enough to read. You always have one ear hanging out because you have to be ready in case you're called."

Appropriately, Ann's first project—and her favorite—is a director's chair. "You know," she says, "like the kind they really use on sets." She found a modern paisley design she liked

Ann B. Davis keeps her director's chair on the set of "The Brady Bunch." On the back she incorporated figures of the television family.

19

in a kit planned as a wall hanging; it happened to be exactly the right size and shape for the chair seat. Not liking all of the colors, she substituted some of her own, using an abundance of hot pinks and purples.

"I made a lot of mistakes, and I didn't know what I was doing," she admits, "but I followed the instructions and asked some questions. You'd be surprised how many people can't wait to help you." When someone pointed out that she ought to be doing it in basketweave, rather than continental, Ann cheerfully changed stitches in mid row. "One more mistake for the better wasn't going to hurt anything," she reasoned, adding modestly, "By the time I finished that seat I was beginning to get a little good at it."

While becoming proficient at her new passion, Ann nevertheless had only the seat half of the director's chair. She still needed both the front and back of the top section. "A friend of mine—in fact, it was the fourteen-year-old daughter of our executive producer—took the general paisley design and used that as the background for both top strips. Real director's chairs usually have your name on them," she explains, "so I did my name in needlepoint on the front section. It's a replica of my signature—somewhat neater, but a replica." On the back section Alice, wearing her white apron, is flanked by stick figures depicting the Brady bunch. Although the seat is done on No. 10 mono canvas, both front and back top sections are stitched on No. 10 penelope, which she split so she could do the Brady figures in petit point.

The finished director's chair is kept on the set of "The Brady Bunch" during the entire shooting season. "And that's where I sit and do more needlepoint while I'm waiting," says Ann. "When the chair 'comes home,' it will just stay some-

Front of Ann B. Davis's director's chair incorporates her signature.

where in the house in readiness to get to the next set!"

Whereas her favorite needlepoint is kept at the studio, Ann is not without finished needlepoint elsewhere. At home she has a pillow of Cancer the crab, which is not her astrology sign. "I'm a Taurus," she reports, "and I simply liked the crab design. I keep looking for a Cancer to give it to." And driving her foreign sports car between home and studio, Ann can enjoy the console cover she upholstered in leopard-print needlepoint.

"I like to have two or three things going at once—in different stages of work," says Ann, "so I can either pay a lot of attention—like sitting in the bright sunlight in the mountains for the weekend and doing my petit point pansy on twenty-four mesh canvas—or I can just pick up my nasturtium pillow and do it without using my head much. If I want to give myself something hard and lose my attention for hours at a time, then I'll get into original stuff like the old English poster, a replica of a pub sign I'm making, which is inscribed: 'Bull and Mouth, fully licensed inn, 1731.' Some patterns give you a chance to do different kinds of things on the same canvas, like the crab pillow that had borders and backgrounds and hard parts, so it stretched to fit any occasion."

The adaptability of needlepoint to many moods is just one of the pleasures Ann finds in it. "One of the most beautiful things is that you don't have to be artistic. No matter how clumsy I was, if I put the needle in the right hole, I made a stitch! I couldn't do it wrong! It's a great thing for me to discover that I can do it. Now I can't put it down," she exclaims. "I just get hysterical about it. It not only kills time on the set, but I come home and work on it two or three hours in the evening because I'm having so much fun."

With such enthusiasm, Ann has inevitably made converts.

Pre-Columbian shards provide inspiration for Kathryn Crosby's needlepoint.

22

A pair of favorite Gauguin paintings reproduced by Rocky Cooper Converse and her daughter Maria Janis.

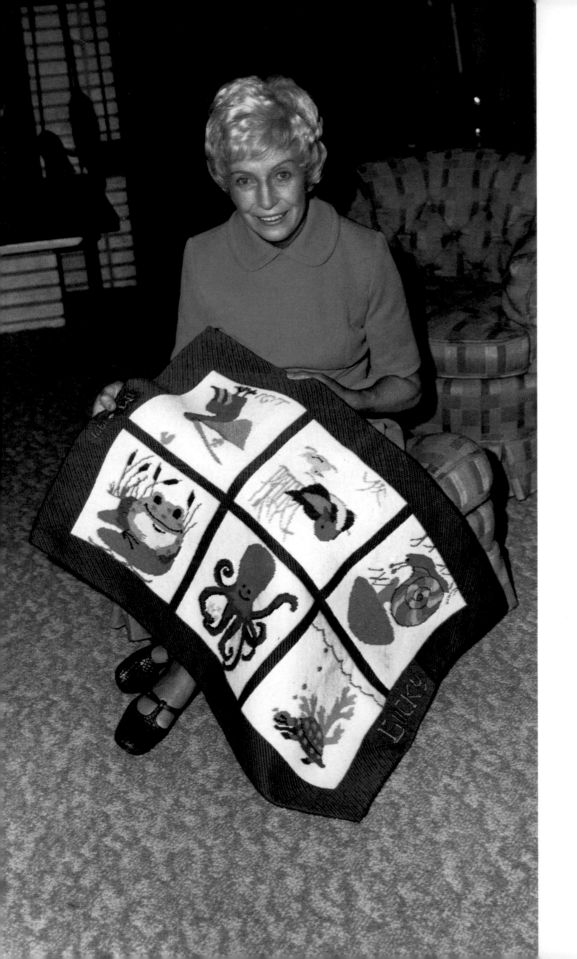

Muriel Humphrey with the water creature rug she made for a grandson.

Roberta Peters made this
bluebird pillow for her library
—called "The Blue Room."

This remarkable table top records some major elements of the lives and accomplishments of Henry and Clare Boothe Luce.

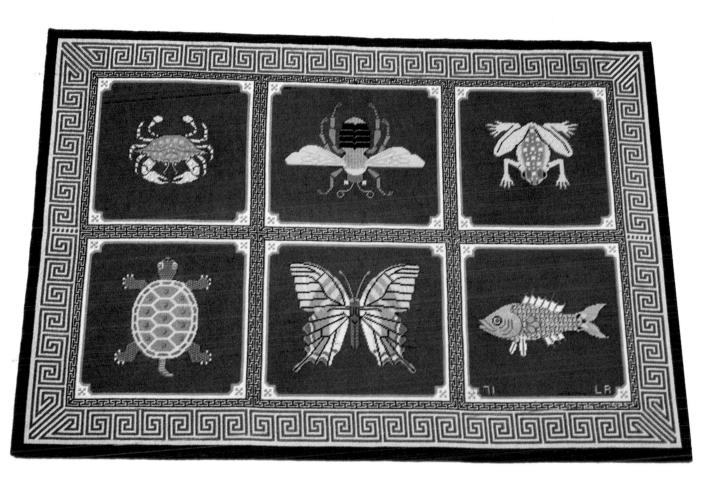

*Lyn Revson combines creatures
of the sea and sky in this rug
based on Maggie Lane designs.*

Leather and needlepoint bedroom slippers, with the presidential seal in gold, a Christmas gift from Mollie Parnis to President Johnson. Photo courtesy Lyndon Baines Johnson Library, Austin, Texas.

"Ruth Buzzi was the one who started me on it, and I started Florence Henderson [her co-star on "The Brady Bunch"]. Everybody starts somebody."

Everybody may start somebody, but few besides Ann B. Davis can claim to have started an entire television set needlepointing. "There are six children in the show, and now they're all playing around with it, including the fellows. Even the little ten-year-old boy has started a rug. The twelve-year-old does all sorts of fancy things such as French knots, much to my delight. He's all boy," Ann reports proudly, "but when he sits down he has this great sense of stitch."

On a typical day at the studio, an electrician sets up a light in the "needlepoint corner" where Ann B. Davis, Florence Henderson, and most of the Brady bunch sit and stitch. "Even on a dark set we have a lighted corner," says Ann. "And when the director says he's ready for us, we're always saying, Wait a minute! Wait a minute! I have to finish this stitch!"

Favorite needlepoint: Director's chair

Design: Adapted by Miss Davis and Hope Schwartz in pale lime green, yellow, gold, orange, purple, hot pink, rose, teal blue, and three browns

Canvas: Seat in No. 10 mono; top sections in No. 10 penelope

Stitches: Basketweave and continental

Julie Eisenhower

Julie Eisenhower's favorite flowers are incorporated into this portion of a wall panel stitched as a gift for her sister Tricia's birthday. The entire panel can be seen in full color facing the title page. Photo courtesy the White House.

For Julie Nixon Eisenhower, only half the fun of needlework is in the stitching. The other half is in giving it away, more than likely as a surprise gift. "I'd like to keep one for myself," she says, "but more often than not, I give my finished work to some member of the family."

Most of Julie's needlework is made surreptitiously, then hidden until an appropriate celebration. This is precisely the case with her favorite—and first—needlepoint, a floral wall panel she made for her sister's birthday, working on it secretly in the White House. Incorporating her favorite flowers in colors to match Tricia's bedroom, the panel was described by Julie as "sort of impressionistic, all multicolored flowers in lavender, pink, green, yellow, and pale orange." It hangs in Tricia's bedroom in the Nixons' San Clemente, California, house.

Julie's first introduction to needlework was through crewel, rather than needlepoint. While still dating David Eisenhower, she admired some crewel pillows his mother, Mrs. John

25

Eisenhower, had stitched, and under the tutelage of her future mother-in-law, Julie learned some basic crewel stitches. She took a piece of crewelwork on her honeymoon. "While David was studying for his exams," she recalls, "I was working on a crewel thing and he didn't know I was making it for him." The surprise present, a wall hanging, was a lion in orange, shocking pink, and purple, with a message that Julie prefers to keep private stitched across the top.

Probably the most public needlework Julie has done was a crewel pillow that she shared with the readers of *Family Circle* magazine. A floral design embroidered on pale beige linen, it depicted bees and butterflies flying through a swirl of spring flowers in a pastel palette of pinks, lavenders, greens, yellows, oranges, and aqua. The pillow design was sold as a mail-order kit, and the profits raised over $80,000 for the Girl Scouts.

Undoubtedly Julie's most famous piece of needlework was the crewelwork presidential seal she stitched for her father during the 1968 campaign. First spotted in a Texas store by her Secret Service agent two months before the election, the kit appealed to her immediately. Julie recalls, "The minute I saw that kit I knew I wanted it. Then I did it secretly for my father, working on it on airplane flights and in the evenings." The seal, which now hangs in the President's White House office, was once displayed at a needlework show. "It was next to a piece of needlepoint Martha Washington had done for one of her nieces," Julie says. "I never felt so complimented in my life."

The great success of the presidential seal has prompted Julie to make another present for her father, this one a needlepoint pillow. Its design is the wreath of peace, stitched in the red and gold colors of the president's bedroom at the San Clemente home. Is she saving it for a special occasion? "Yes," she admits, "for his birthday or Christmas—depending on when it's finished."

Favorite needlepoint: Floral wall panel, approximately thirteen inches square

Design: Painted on canvas, in lavender, pink, green, yellow, and pale orange

Canvas: No. 10 mono

Stitch: Continental

Joan Fontaine

Joan Fontaine's favorite is an ocelot, painted for her on needlepoint canvas by Salvador Dali.

"Some people air-cool cellars for their wine. I air-condition my apartment for my needlepoint," says Joan Fontaine laughingly. The care she takes of her needlepoint is not misplaced, for one piece is a unique and probably priceless canvas painted for her by Salvador Dali. Not surprisingly, it is her favorite.

"The only place I can work on it is right here in this room," she says, indicating her paneled library with its antique furniture and shelves of signed and well-read books. "The canvas is only partially finished," she explains. "I can't do it on trains and planes because I might lose it."

The Dali needlepoint, a gift from the artist, depicts his pet ocelot who accompanies him everywhere. The ocelot stays at the St. Regis Hotel in New York with Dali, goes to restaurants with him, visits friends, and has, in fact, been to Miss Fontaine's apartment. "He came here one day, liked the house, and," she recalls, pointing to a corner of the room, "hid right there. Hostesses are so pleased to have Mr. Dali around that they'll take an elephant," she adds with a laugh.

29

It was after this visit that Dali painted his pet's portrait for her on a needlepoint canvas, incorporating his signature as an integral part of the design. "It's interesting, isn't it—rather like a butterfly," she remarks. "It's been fascinating to do, and he chose the colors as well. If it were a painting, think of the price, but a *needlepoint* canvas! I don't think he's ever done one before. Wasn't that an extraordinary gesture of friendship!"

When finished, the canvas will be framed under glass. "Dali probably wanted it for a seat," says Miss Fontaine, indicating a set of needlepoint chair seats with animal head designs, "but I'm going to do it as a painting, and its worth will be astronomical." She has had a copy of the ocelot painted, which she will stitch for a chair cover after the original is completed.

Needlework has been an avocation of Joan Fontaine's since childhood days in a convent school. "We were taught exquisite needlework: embroidery, appliqué, everything. If your darning was bad, you had to cut it out and do it all over again. I loved it. All the other girls gave me their darning to do." She has since tried beading, knitting, and weaving, but now concentrates primarily on needlepoint, although she would love to do other crafts. "It's a problem of time. I don't stay home much—and I don't look at TV often, though I find needlepoint a wonderful way of watching those football or golf games or whatever you have to see to be a good sport."

Most of her needlepoint is done when traveling and acting. "Needlepoint is the loveliest thing to do on a set when waiting for the lighting," she explains. "Gossip and cigarettes are not good for acting, so I found I could do this without looking aloof and shut off. The workmen still come and talk to you, and it's very useful and calming."

30

Backstage with a play is another ideal place to stitch, "though only," Miss Fontaine cautions, "if you're not on all the time. Otherwise you make mistakes or get the yarn dirty with make-up." One perfect play for stitching is *Dial M for Murder*, which Miss Fontaine has played several times, most recently on a South African tour. "I only come on once in the first act, so I know I'm going to have a whole act in which to work on a canvas." During one run she stitched a design of primitive jungle animals. "Looking at that pillow," she says, "I can recall the dialogue as I sat in the dressing room waiting to go on."

Other vivid memories, too, are often revived by a finished piece of needlepoint. Miss Fontaine points to a pillow incorporating a variety of sea creatures and shells, which she worked on during a trip to Iran when she fell victim to a terrible attack of "Teheran tummy." "Night and day, with a temperature of 104 or 105 degrees, I did the needlepoint," she recalls. "Every time I look at that pillow, I feel the fever and see the view from the hotel window. Stitching is good for bad times," she observes. "It steadies your nerves, and gives you a little sense of tranquillity, a pause that, perhaps, makes you think a little more clearly."

With needlework such a consistent part of her life, it is not surprising that Miss Fontaine has produced finished objects in quantity and variety: rugs, pillows, chair seats, eyeglass cases, and picture frames, which, she explains, are mounted so expertly they don't look handmade. "I gave one to George Cukor, the director, but I don't think to this day he believes I made it," she says with mock indignation.

"I think that's the only thing I ever gave away," she continues reminiscently, "—except for shoes. Most of the men in my life have been wearing beautiful needlepoint slippers." She designs her own patterns for these. "I've found that patchwork is such fun to do for men's shoes. You can use up all your old yarn and invent the most extraordinary stitches and patterns, just by going ahead and doing squares and rectangles and triangles. Of course, I've done initials and all kinds of designs in addition to the patchwork."

Aside from a large floral rug in the living room, the most ambitious project she has stitched is a set of seats for the sixteenth- and seventeenth-century mahogany chairs in the study and dining room. A giraffe, tiger, zebra, lion, and leopard are viewed head-on, each face centered on a seat and surrounded by its skin marking. "I'm inclined to get a little rosebuddy," she says in explanation of the choice of jungle designs, "and since the chairs are rather masculine, I thought it would be nice to do them in a kind of mannish way so the room didn't get to be a feminine nook."

These were the animal seat covers that originally inspired the Dali design. Contemplating that favorite piece of needlepoint appreciatively, Miss Fontaine remarks, "It's so beautiful I couldn't use it as a seat, of course. I'm going to frame it, put it under glass, and leave it to a museum. Really a present, isn't it!"

Favorite needlepoint: Painting of Salvador Dali's pet ocelot, twenty by twenty-four inches

Design: By Salvador Dali

Canvas: No. 14 mono

Stitch: Basketweave

Betty Furness

Betty Furness lives in a delightful saltbox colonial house, painted barn red and backed by a grove of trees. Inside, comfort and order prevail in rooms filled with books, beautiful objects, a harmonious melange of colors and patterns, and an abundance of needlepoint.

Her successful years as actress, commercial spokeswoman, and more recently, consumer ombudsman and columnist for *McCall's* magazine have left Miss Furness with a penchant for never doing less than two things simultaneously, an approach she also applies to stitchery. "Sitting down to do needlepoint in the daytime without any other occupation seems to me like drinking in the morning," she says with all the force of her New England heritage.

The same background compelled her, after a thirty-two-year hiatus, to complete the piece of needlepoint she now considers her favorite. It is a dove pillow that she began in 1937, found too difficult at the time, and put away carefully with accompanying wool for the intervening years. "I'm a little bit of a procrastinator," she says with a smile, "but I'm definitely a string saver. My New England conscience finally made me finish it." Completed, the pillow has been a prize exhibit in needlework shows around the country, surely an inspiration to anyone else who has been postponing work on a too-difficult piece.

Miss Furness's hands were by no means idle during the interval when the dove canvas nagged at her conscience. Although she had dropped needlepoint for a period of years, she always kept a stitchery project of some kind, explaining, "I've been working with my hands since I was fourteen. I knitted a lot," she recalls of her early Hollywood days, "and taught many people out there. I think I even taught Joan Crawford."

Once Miss Furness returned to needlepoint, however, with a lion and unicorn canvas in 1950, she channeled her enthusiasm for handwork almost exclusively into canvas work. "I have no interest in crewel," she remarks. "It's more creative than I mean to be. I can't do original designs, but I like color —like to look at colors—so needlepoint is ideal for me. Although I'm not creative, I'm a very good mechanic and I like to count." With perceptive self-analysis, she continues, "It's all in temperament. As it relaxes me, it makes other people nervous. I like to whip through, which is why I get so much pleasure from bargello. It's fun because it goes so fast."

Betty Furness's predilection for speed and doing two things at once has combined to produce an astounding quantity of finished projects—a total of eighty-seven pieces. In the living room, a large, handsome needlepoint rug keynotes the color scheme. It was made when she was moving into a New York City apartment. She states, "First I made it, then had no place

*A prettily fringed pillow with
a dove of peace bearing an olive
branch is Betty Furness's
favorite.*

Betty Furness works one of her favorite bargello patterns.

to put it. So I decorated a room around it." When she moved to her present suburban house, she searched for a floor covering for the library, and finally realized that the needlepoint rug was perfect. In the same book-lined room, a striking, multiflowered fire screen stands in front of the fireplace. Needlepoint pillows are scattered with a lavish hand, another needlepoint rug decorates the front hall, and still the surface of her productivity is barely scratched.

Betty Furness's library is a showcase for her unusual needlepoint rug and firescreen.

"I don't love giving needlepoint away," she laughs. "I *have* to give it away. I make all these for the pleasure of working on them," she says, spreading out half a dozen jewel-toned bargellos, ready to cover pillows as gifts to special friends. For Joe Eula, the noted fashion artist, she copied a cheetah he had drawn as a nightclub trademark. For Kenneth, the hairdresser and her friend, she made stair treads for a circular library stepladder, stitching stylized numbers in browns and beiges. The treads were designed by Jules Tomchin, as was a pillow she made for author Robert Crichton when his book, *The Secret of Santa Vittoria*, was published. She covered a large pillow with the opening phrases of a *New York Times* review which said that the book calls for "fanfares of trumpets, display of banners, and festivals in the streets . . ." Says Miss Furness, "It described exactly how all his friends felt when the book was published."

Obviously, canvases in work frequently accompany Miss Furness. "I do needlepoint on planes or at the hairdresser. I do it socially. I may take along my needlepoint to a good friend's house if I know she needlepoints, too. I think most men would rather we wouldn't do it. They think we're not giving them total attention. But my husband doesn't complain. And you learn to save complicated things to work on when you're alone." A favorite spot for needlepointing is a corner of the sofa

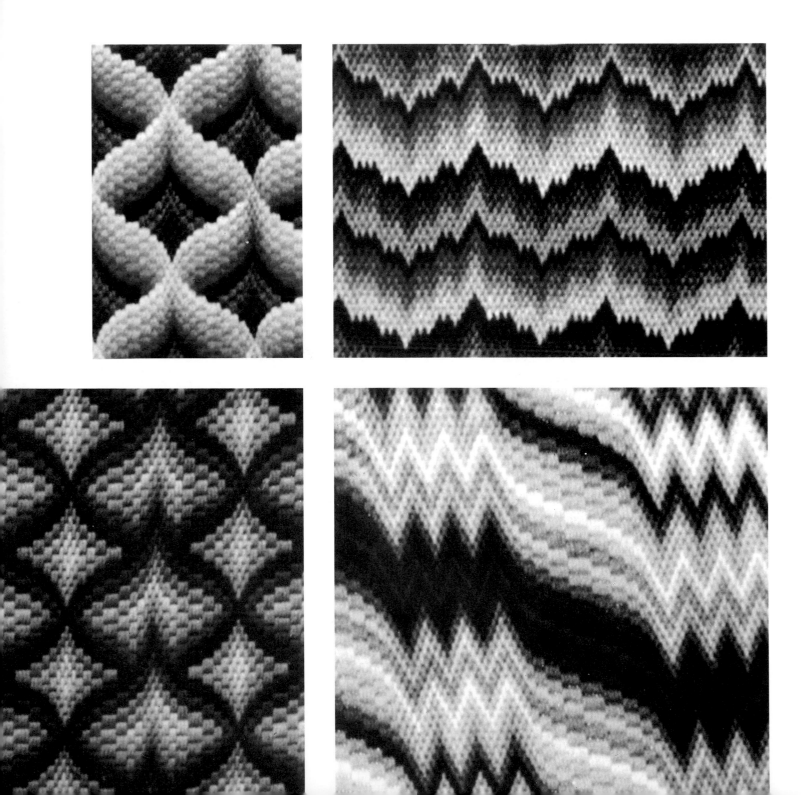

Details from Betty Furness's bargello. She sometimes stitches the same bargello pattern in various color schemes to create entirely different effects. These patterns can be seen in full color in the insert following page 86.

by an enormous brick fireplace, where a large basket holds a variety of canvases and wools, and Miss Furness can watch the evening news with her husband, Leslie Midgley, a CBS television news executive.

Years of enthusiastic stitching have provided Miss Furness with advice for the beginner: "I'd tell a novice to start on a small, ready-made design, but not one with the pattern worked and just the background to fill in. That's cheating beyond belief. Starting on something too large or too challenging can turn you off the whole hobby." For those who have reached a more advanced stage, she advises on managing bulky pieces, such as a one-piece rug, "Roll both ends toward the middle, pinning the rolls with a big safety pin; then start in the middle and work out to the ends." Finally, in addition to having a non-needlepointing occupation going at the same time, she also recommends simultaneous canvas projects. "Most people like to have two things in work at once—something hard and something easy, harder work to be done in daylight with no interruptions, easier work to be done while talking or watching TV.

Favorite needlepoint: Dove pillow, twelve- by fourteen-inch oval

Design: Gray dove on pink background with leaf wreath as border

Canvas: No. 16 mono

Stitch: Basketweave

A pillow with a pair of Chinese geese is proudly displayed by Hermione Gingold. Each of the butterfly pillows behind her is stitched in a different color.

Hermione Gingold

When Hermione Gingold appears "on stage" in her New York City apartment, it is immediately apparent that the veteran comedienne delights in being outrageous. "I don't think I should be seen doing anything useful," she drawls archly in her familiar British accent, admitting only reluctantly to such practical accomplishments as marbling furniture, cooking ("I make fettucine, stew, and a marvelous mousse"), and needlepoint.

Her stitching began on the set of the movie *Gigi*. "I think Leslie Caron was doing needlepoint, and I had to do something while waiting on the set," Miss Gingold recalls. "I do most of my work while lights are being placed, when I find it very relaxing. I'm not of a nervous temperament, but it helps on a set where you can get very nervy waiting about."

Quickly convinced of the therapeutic properties of needlepoint, Miss Gingold introduced a number of fellow actors to her new accomplishment. "I taught the director of *Auntie Mame* and a number of other men," she relates with obvious relish, wishing that she could include her co-star the late Maurice Chevalier's name for its shock value alone. She even persuaded her doctor to do it, prescribing for him instead of the other way round.

Her first needlepoint project is still her favorite: a rug for her bedroom made up of twenty-four squares with the official flowers of twenty-four states in America where she has toured. Since most novices start with something small, she is often asked what prompted her to begin with a rug. "But I'm ambitious!" is her droll answer.

Other needlepoint decorates her Manhattan apartment,

Hermione Gingold's favorite is this rug, incorporating the official flowers of twenty-four states where she has toured.

Details from the rug above by Hermione Gingold.

Hermione Gingold's Yorkshire terrier poses in front of the butterfly pillows.

which is a crowded repository for paintings and furniture from a large house Miss Gingold left in London. Tours for various charities often come through the apartment. "I think they're fascinated to see where the wicked Miss Gingold lives," she remarks slyly. The decorating is as fantastic and intriguing as Miss Gingold herself. Green palms nod beside blackamoor statues, primitive paintings hang on the walls, and Regency antiques seem perfectly at home with fur rugs, bowls of cabbage roses, and a pair of yellow needlepoint pillows decorated with climbing monkeys. "Don't you think they're amusing?" she asks.

Miss Gingold buys many of her canvases in London, because they are cheaper there and not seen everywhere here; she works in the continental stitch only. "I tried to learn the others," she explains, "but I couldn't be bothered." One problem was her Yorkshire terrier's insistence on sitting on her lap when she was working, "which makes it rather difficult."

Despite her own enjoyment of needlepoint, Miss Gingold has strong feelings against stitching while watching television. "When I watch TV, I *watch*. Since I play on TV myself, I resent it that people are stitching or playing bridge while I'm sweating my guts out to entertain them. That's a bore!"

Favorite needlepoint: State flower rug, sixty-four by ninety-six inches; twenty-four sixteen-inch squares, each with an official state flower

Design: Alice Maynard, New York

Canvas: No. 8 penelope

Stitch: Continental

Princess Grace of Monaco

When Grace Kelly married Prince Rainier in the romantic fairy-tale wedding of the century, a few practical souls wondered how an American girl would adjust to the role of reigning royalty. As if to the palace born, is the obvious answer by now.

Princess Grace credits self-discipline for the apparent ease with which she has adjusted to her demanding royal duties. She traces this strong sense of discipline both to her career as an actress and to earlier years in a Philadelphia convent school under French nuns (where she now laughingly wishes she had paid closer attention to French lessons).

And for relaxation— just as you and I—she needlepoints.

"I've always loved doing needlepoint," remembers Princess Grace. "I started as a child with the help of my mother [Mrs. John B. Kelly]. Now I carry a canvas with me as often as possible. I bring needlepoint with me when traveling, and I may work when talking with the Prince or with friends in the

Princess Grace of Monaco in the palace gardens. Photo courtesy Tom Hustler, London.

evenings or at tea time—if my busy schedule permits it. I hate sitting and doing nothing."

During her years in Monaco, Her Serene Highness has produced an enormous variety of needlepoint projects. She has particularly enjoyed making gifts for family and friends. A delightful rug that she stitched for her younger daughter depicts characters from *Winnie the Pooh* and is signed affectionately, "To Stephanie—With Love—From Mother." For the Prince she made a pair of slippers. She has made pillows and

Princess Grace's favorite is a petit point vest she stitched for Prince Rainier.

cushions for her mother and her friends, and, like thrifty needlewomen the world over, she often stitches small pieces such as luggage-rack straps in order to use up leftover yarns. From all her needlepoint the Princess has picked as her favorite a waistcoat she made for Prince Rainier a few years ago, which, she says, "was the hardest." Stitched in petit point, the vest has a profusion of tiny field flowers sprinkled over a wine-colored background.

Although much of her needlepoint is custom designed in shops in New York and Paris, Princess Grace has designed many pieces herself and finds it particular fun to copy paintings. "I recently reproduced in needlepoint one by my friend Fleur Cowles," she says. She has also made some of the Raffaelo patterns of old Florentine embroidery. The Princess prefers mono canvas, varying the size of the mesh to suit each particular project. She generally uses wool yarn, but occasionally combines it with silk for special effects.

Favorite needlepoint: Petit point waistcoat for Prince Rainier

Design: By Mazaltov's, Inc., New York; pink, blue, and white flowers on a wine background

Canvas: No. 16 mono

Stitch: Basketweave

Rosey Grier

"From he-man to sissy," is the crack that Rosey Grier reports old friends make about his enthusiasm for needlepoint. But those are close friends. Strangers who might consider stitchery an incongruous pastime for the six-foot five-inch, three-hundred-pound ex-professional football star might very well keep their opinions to themselves.

"My old football pals think it's funny," Rosey admits, but he plans to turn the tables on them. "I'm working on some of those guys to get *them* to needlepoint—guys like Ben Wilson and Alvin Hall [former fullback and defensive back, respectively, for the Los Angeles Rams]."

With a successful sports career behind him, followed by equal success in his current entertainment pursuits as actor, songwriter, performer and recording artist, talk-show host, and frequent television guest (when he occasionally needlepoints on camera), Rosey Grier wastes little time worrying about other people's opinions of his hobby. "A lot of times when

Rosey Grier finds time to needlepoint, even at the tennis court. Photo by James Roark.

One of Rosey Grier's current projects is a black-and-white caricature of himself contemplating a rose. Photo courtesy Petit Point Junction, Los Angeles.

you're thinking about things and you want to settle yourself down or calm yourself, it takes your mind off a particular thing and relaxes you," he explains. He has no particular routine for needlepoint. "I do it at night or in the day—whenever I feel like it."

It all began at Jebba's needlepoint shop in Beverly Hills. "I was fooling around, pretending I knew what I was doing and telling Willie Shoemaker's wife, Babs, that she was needlepointing all wrong," Rosey remembers. "Then I asked if they would show me a few things so I could really talk about it, and I became interested."

He went on to make a belt with stars and stripes, a tennis

51

racquet cover featuring two large sneakers, and a pillow with facing lions. These were all for himself. "I haven't made any gifts yet," Rosey says. "I just want to do stuff for myself now. Maybe I'll do things for other people later on when I've done more of it. I'm thinking of trying faces of people—caricatures —next. That's a very interesting and challenging thing." His first face may very well be his own, since he was given a needlepoint canvas painted with a caricature of himself, beard and all, smelling a rose, with a tiny football hovering over the "i" in his name.

Meanwhile, Rosey's favorite needlepoint to date is an animal rug currently in progress. The first section depicts three

Rosey Grier's favorite, "Duck-Duck," will be part of an animal rug. He stitched it in black, white, blue, and mustard brown. Photo courtesy Jebba, Inc., Los Angeles.

ducks walking along a beach with their reflections cast in the water. The rug will eventually include twelve sections, with a group of tame or jungle animals in each segment.

Favorite needlepoint: "Duck Duck," fourteen by twenty inches, a section for an animal rug

Design: Painted by Jebba, Inc., Los Angeles, California, in black, white, blue, and mustard brown

Canvas: No. 12 mono

Stitch: Continental

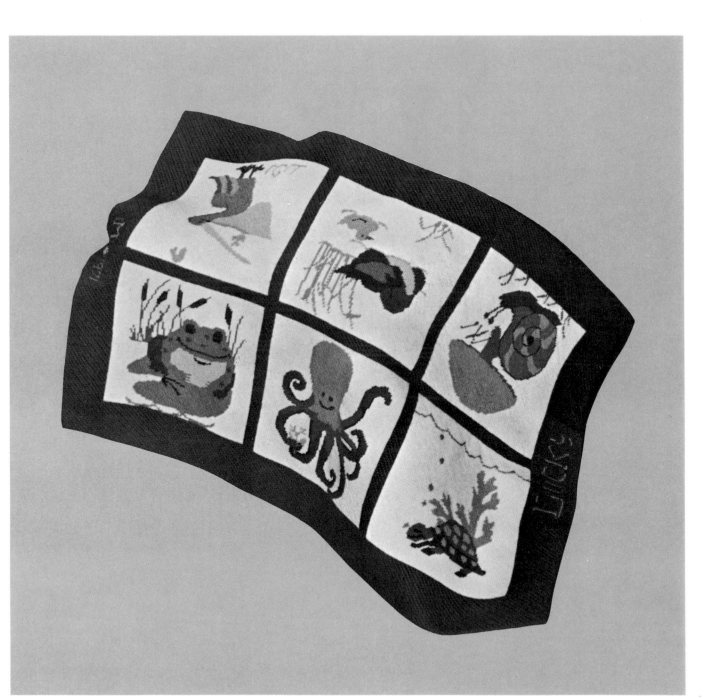

Muriel Humphrey

A veteran campaigner and Washington hostess, never far from the center of political action, Muriel Humphrey takes equal delight in another role when she plies her needle—that of doting grandmother. Most of her needlepoint output goes for the pleasure of her eight grandchildren and their families.

For her six granddaughters, Mrs. Humphrey has made needlepoint pillows, each in a different flower pattern stitched with the child's name. "Jill" and "Vicky," for instance, are wreathed by flowers. "Amy" is in the right corner, gazing out on a spray of spring flowers that includes day lilies, daffodils, and bluebells.

It was while planning a needlepoint project for one of her sons that Muriel Humphrey came across the idea for the piece that is now her favorite—a child's rug for her first grandson, Hubert H. Humphrey, IV, also known as Bucky. The rug is made of six squares of "water creatures": frog, snail, pelican, octopus, turtle, and mother and baby duck.

Animal creature rug made by Muriel Humphrey for a grandson.

55

"It's my own design," explains Mrs. Humphrey. "I was looking through a children's coloring book for a design for my son who loves turtles, and ran across all of these wonderful animals. I put the design on canvas myself. I drew them directly onto the canvas with a No. 2 lead pencil, using a combination of freehand and copying."

Although Mrs. Humphrey has used oil and acrylic paints on her needlepoint designs, she has also had success with crayons, which she used to color in this particular design. "When the coloring is finished, I press it on an ironing board with a cloth to absorb the oils of the crayons and to protect the canvas from the hot iron. I prefer a hot, not a warm, iron so that all the oils are absorbed."

The two- by three-foot rug was stitched in one piece, with each of the water creatures done in a variety of colors on a white background and framed in a midnight blue border. Pinks, purples, greens, and blues predominate, with occasional touches of oranges and yellows. "I like the whimsical warmth and happiness in the colors I've chosen, plus the expression of the creatures," says Mrs. Humphrey. "It was fun to do—probably the most fun piece I have ever done." She adds fondly, "I hope it will be something Bucky will treasure the rest of his life."

Mrs. Humphrey's interest in needlepoint was natural, since, she explains, "I'm happier if I'm busy with my hands. A friend helped me get started," she recalls. "I had always loved sewing, but found that I couldn't take my work with me as easily as I could needlepoint. So I have largely shifted to needlepoint and don't sew as many clothes and articles as I once did."

With portability a top priority, needlepoint fits very well

into Mrs. Humphrey's exceedingly busy life. "I generally work on several pieces at a time. I carry them with me where I go —the hospital, vacation, traveling with my husband. The rug was a little large to handle on a plane, but I have even worked on it there." Currently accompanying Mrs. Humphrey are bargello designs for two footstools, a bench cover for her daughter, and another animal rug for her second grandson, undoubtedly inspired by the smashing success of the first.

Wherever Mrs. Humphrey travels, she is on the lookout for needlepoint. "I like the yarn I found in London," she reports, "and the Clara Waever designs in Copenhagen are among my favorites. But in many different cities, in the United States as well as elsewhere, I have found many good designers —and unfortunately, poor designers, too."

Whether it's the scarcity of good design or the fun of creating distinctively individual patterns, Mrs. Humphrey is turning more frequently to designing her own needlepoint. "I'm still a novice at designing," she says modestly, "and try many things in both geometric and traditional styles. I may be inspired by a modern painting or a special interest of one of our children. For example, our son Doug loves the outdoors and wildlife, so I tried to reflect this interest in the needlepoint I did for him. Sometimes I draw freehand directly onto the canvas, but when I do geometric designs, I carefully draw them on graph paper first and then transfer them to the canvas."

With an enthusiastic interest in needlepoint, Mrs. Humphrey happily passes on some tips she has accumulated, some of them the hard way:

"Never, never use an ordinary felt pen in transferring designs. One must be careful whatever materials are used in the designs to test them first for waterproofing. They must be permanent and waterproof. If you make a mistake one time, as I have, you never will again.

"Read as much as you can about the art of needlepoint, because it is an ancient and an honored art, and visit needlepoint displays and exhibits. It is helpful to learn as much as possible about what others are doing, so that you can determine your own preferences.

"Be aware and careful about the quality of the canvas and yarn which are purchased. You are going to put in many hours of work on it and you want the finished product to be something that you can be proud of for many years."

Mrs. Humphrey is the first to take her own advice, confessing, "I'm a perfectionist about the work and make my pieces with the hope that they will be treasured—and many years from now regarded as family heirlooms." Meanwhile, they are enjoyed by the entire Humphrey clan, and not least by Mrs. Humphrey herself, who says, "Needlepoint is one of the most exciting, satisfying and creative things that I have ever done in my life."

Favorite needlepoint: Water Creatures rug, two feet by three feet

Design: By Mrs. Humphrey

Canvas: No. 10 mono

Stitches: Animal squares in basketweave; border in diagonal mosaic

Melanie Kahane

The pronouncement, "Needlepoint in a room can be the personal hallmark of a woman," is hard to challenge when it comes from a world authority on décor such as Melanie Kahane. "I think it's extraordinary that we have a period of handcrafts again," the noted interior designer comments with evident approval. "People are desperate for the fineness, the tactile quality of the handmade."

Miss Kahane, who has given decorating advice to governments and industry as well as to a long list of discerning individuals, has firm opinions on the place of needlepoint in a home. "For a client, we may suggest a needlepoint design inspired by a piece of print fabric, or a pattern might be taken from the edge of a piece of antique china—Copeland or Imari ware, for instance. For a Boston client with an important collection of Impressionist paintings, we even picked out needlepoint yarns so she would have the right colors to stitch a pillow as an accent in her home."

As for the backing of needlepoint pillows, "anything goes," according to Miss Kahane. "Ticking, velvet, felt, suede. Even the back of a flour sack if it were right . . ." she begins, then quickly corrects herself. "No, that's absurd. But color is the important thing."

Although she adores pillows, Miss Kahane particularly likes less familiar uses for needlepoint. "It would be marvelous to cover a tiny chair next to a telephone in the bedroom, or a dressing table bench or a footstool, using a pattern like gingham or a small allover design instead of a pretentious one," she suggests. "Another wonderful needlepoint idea would be trompe l'oeil tiebacks—a simple rope design with a large metal ring for a gutsy look on plain draperies. Picture frames can be enchanting—again, trompe l'oeil, or a three-dimensional shadow effect to give depth. And needlepoint seats for dining room chairs can be chic. All the wood in a dining room needs that warmth."

As rapidly as the ideas flow, Miss Kahane intersperses warnings: "Avoid little picky things like wreaths. Or those medallions which I loathe." She feels, also, that it's entirely possible to overload a room with handiwork. "Women can get too much needlepoint in a room. I call it therapeutic hysteria when they limit their creativity to needlepoint and go overboard. A room too filled with it can become bloated. This diminishes the quality. Too much of anything is too much."

In the living room of her handsome town house she displays her handwork sparingly. A crewel unicorn and a needlepoint pillow with a black and white skunk sniffing a pumpkin-colored flower (a color scheme, incidentally, for which she is famous) rest on the sofa, in front of a rare and superb Coro-

Melanie Kahane's turtle design adorns the top of an antique Louis XVI bench.

mandel screen. The eclectic mixture of French and Oriental antiques betrays a lively interest in many art forms that she shares with her husband, NBC commentator Ben Grauer. "My husband and I are both hopeless collectors," she acknowledges, indicating a group of eighteenth-century gold snuff boxes, pre-Columbian figures, Etruscan and Punic artifacts, and even an antique bit of embroidery from Yugoslavia.

Another major Kahane warning to needlepointers is: "Avoid the predictable. The penalty of decorating in the early thirties, for instance, was that you could walk into a room looking for the mirror above the fireplace, the two club chairs, and the breakfront on the opposite wall. The same predictability has stigmatized needlework."

She describes her own solution to this problem as she rummages in a large canvas tote bag filled with a variety of creative projects and pulls out her favorite, a needlepoint turtle worked in a variety of stitches—brick, Smyrna cross, double leviathan, upright cross, and basketweave—and destined to be a cushion for an antique eighteenth century Louis XVI bench. She explains, "I like a difference in texture, different stitches, colors. That way, you don't get that static needlepoint look of all one stitch. Needlepoint should be an exquisite rhythm of textures and different stitches."

Favorite needlepoint: Turtle bench cushion, thirteen inches square, two-and-one-half inches high

Design: Adapted from Maggie Lane, in brick red, navy, emerald green, sage green, pale gray, and white

Melanie Kahane at work.

Canvas: No. 12 mono

Stitches: Brick for background, double leviathan for bumps on turtle, Smyrna cross for smaller bumps on border, upright cross for turtle's hands and feet, and basketweave for remainder of turtle and border

Abbe Lane

"I go berserk in a needlepoint shop, like a child in a candy store," admits Abbe Lane, perhaps to the surprise of some fans who find it hard to picture the glamorous television and night-club star in so domestic a role.

"I'm very romantic and old-fashioned in my style in needlepoint," Abbe continues, as she points out her favorite, a flowered antique footstool. She chose the design because it was typical of the old-fashioned European kind of pattern and began stitching it over three years ago. "I worked on it for a time, then put it down for a while," she recalls. "I had bought the canvas without owning a stool, and although the shop had a reproduction to fit it, I was determined to find an antique. And that really took a lot of doing. The stool I finally got was a little bit larger than the pattern, so I had to fill in at least three-quarters of an inch all around by reproducing the pattern free-hand." Once finished, the footstool was moved from room to room, and is now settled comfortably with a chair by the fire-

place in Abbe's bedroom. "It's the kind of stool that could go from house to house very easily and always find a room," Abbe says approvingly.

"Like most people who enjoy needlepoint, I never have just one thing going at a time," she continues. "You get tired of working on the same piece, or your eyes begin to hurt after a while, so you switch canvases." Among her current projects are a pillow with a large camel and two small petit point canvases, one with violets, the other a bunch of mixed wild flowers. "They were originally meant to be framed, but I usually don't like to frame things," Abbe says, "so I think I'm going to make

A charming floral design mounted on an antique footstool is Abbe Lane's favorite. The rust and green flowers and gold ribbon are stitched on a beige field.

66

The vivid colors of this elephant's head and the unusual side tasseling make a striking pillow accent in Abbe Lane's living room.

two very, very tiny pillows for the bedroom. I am also in the middle of a piano bench cushion with old instruments—a lute, a harpsichord. Again, it leads to the old and the romantic."

Another, more ambitious project simultaneously under way is a needlepoint rug. "I bought a hooked rug pattern in a fantastic Oriental design," Abbe says, "but I'm needlepointing, not hooking it, using a cross stitch. It's a true Oriental design taken from an old pattern and it was so cheap I couldn't believe it. Of course, you use a lot of wool doing the cross stitch, but it gives it a marvelous heavy texture."

Needlepointing a rug is coming full circle for Abbe, since

67

her first project was a rug for her children. "It's all animals," she explains, "about two-and-one-half by three feet, with elephant, giraffe, pelican, hippopotamus, monkey, and tiger. It hangs on the wall now because the children are so young. It was a large project and I finished it during my first pregnancy because I was forced to spend a lot of time indoors and had nothing to do to distract me. But I really couldn't wait until it was finished."

Abbe cautions other needlepoint novices against following her example. "Start with a small simple piece, something relatively inexpensive and easy to do. When you've learned the different stitches, then work your way up. I think most people, and especially beginners, like to see their work finished and displayed—then they have the inspiration to go on to something else."

Abbe herself obviously wasn't daunted by an overly ambitious dive into needlepoint, and she has since made the hobby an integral part of her life. "I do it everywhere," she says. "On planes, on sets, and often when we're visiting with friends. After dinner it's a very quiet, private thing while the men play pool. It's marvelous therapy," she adds, "and very creative."

With such enthusiasm, Abbe has completed a large array of projects in the few years since she's taken up canvas work. Needlepoint and bargello pillows provide striking color accents on the black and white couches in her Beverly Hills living room. "And I've given a lot away," she says. "When Barbra Streisand came out to do *Funny Girl*, I gave her a pillow with an art deco figure for her dressing room. Barbara Rush loves to putter in her garden, so I made her one with flowers. For my husband [television executive Perry Leff], I made a pair of slippers in petit and gros point. The entire eagle on the front was done in silk thread from England, almost impossible to work with because it sticks to your fingers and everything else."

A gift for herself is a pillow with luscious flowers in the background and in the center—MERDE. "I bought that because there are mornings when I wake up and that's just the way I feel."

With all these projects completed or in the works, Abbe still bubbles with excitement about her future needlepoint plans. "I do research in old art books on the designs I like myself. There's a big bowl of flowers—marvelous flowers—painted by Cézanne that I cut out of a magazine and I'm going to have it reproduced. I would like to hang that. And when I'm through with all my other things, I think I'd like to do some seats for my dining room. I've sketched an idea I have, but that's a big project, and I don't want to get started on it until I finish what I have," she says firmly. "I feel guilty because in my needlepoint closet there are bags and bags and bags of different things all calling for my attention!"

Favorite needlepoint: Floral footstool, fifteen- by eighteen-inch oval

Design: By Mazaltov, Inc., New York, in green, yellows, and light rust on beige background

Canvas: No. 14 mono

Stitches: Flowers in continental, background in basketweave

Janet Leigh

The easy portability of canvas work and its compatibility with other activities was clearly demonstrated recently by Janet Leigh, a new and enthusiastic convert to the craft. "I even took my needlepoint on the Johnny Carson show," she reports. Asked how she could concentrate on what she said, how she looked, and where she stitched—all at the same time—she explains, "I just think about what I'm saying. Once you get into needlepointing, it goes along almost automatically."

Miss Leigh began the craft as part of a deliberate effort to cut down on smoking. "I started because I wanted to have something to do instead of smoking when I was sitting around and talking. Now I work on my needlepoint on the set between shots when I have time, as well as at home when I'm talking with my husband."

Janet Leigh chose a Matisse design and stitched the leaves in green, orange, red, yellow, and blue.

Miss Leigh's favorite needlepoint is her first—a gay and colorful rendering of swirling leaves in familiar Matisse-like shapes and colors. A mass of orange, yellow, fuchsia, blue, and green leaves tumble on a white background, caught in a simple box frame of a matching bitter green color. The square needlepoint panel, measuring seventeen by seventeen inches, hangs by her bed, an appropriate gallery companion to the Jackson Pollock and Helen Frankenthaler posters mounted nearby on the white walls of the room.

The clean, bold lines of the Matisse-inspired needlepoint reflect the contemporary, spacious feeling in her hillside house high in Beverly Hills. In the large circular living room, polished wood walls are generously hung with a varied collection of modern art. A semicircle of oversized couches, plumped with an abundance of striped pillows, faces an indoor garden, a sweep of pool and terrace, and a spectacular view of Los Angeles below.

Despite her affection for pillows, Miss Leigh has not yet made any out of needlepoint. Her second stitching project, made to be framed like the first, was a gift for a friend based on a love theme. Her third and current one is a two-sided tote bag incorporating ducks and birds in the design. Like the first two pieces she made, its design was painted on a large-mesh canvas and purchased ready-made.

Needlepoint shares Miss Leigh's attention with her many other interests. She is an avid tennis player and skier, even sponsoring her own ski tournament, and spends much time in outdoor sports with her two teen-age daughters and husband. "To be married to my husband," she says, "you have to become an expert skier, boater, camper, and, of course, tennis player."

She has already made over forty movies and many television films and guest appearances. When interviewed, Miss Leigh was in make-up, ready to resume work on her newest film, with canvas, wool, and needle at the ready for the long waits that are part of film making. "I haven't entirely given up cigarettes for needlepoint yet," she says in a tone of regret. "But it's helped me cut back."

Favorite needlepoint: "Leaves," based on a Matisse design

Design: Adapted by Haystack, Ltd., Beverly Hills, California

Canvas: No. 5 penelope

Stitch: Half cross

Clare Boothe Luce

Details from a tabletop by Clare Boothe Luce depict aspects of her life and that of her husband Henry Luce. The tabletop can be seen in full color in the insert following page 86.

Clare Boothe Luce, author, playwright, columnist, Congresswoman, and Ambassador, is articulate, witty, and outspoken on virtually every aspect of the human condition. She has even, on occasion, turned an appraising eye on stitchery.

Needlework is a creative hobby that has survived the inroads of the machine, Mrs. Luce believes.

"Creative." That's the controlling word. Mrs. Luce has little sympathy for the unimaginative, the pedestrian, and especially not for mass-produced, store-bought designs that stifle creativity.

With such a standard for excellence in needlepoint, Mrs. Luce might well be describing the piece that is her own favorite, for it meets a basic condition: it is a perfect and precise rendition of an original design. An amateur artist, she designed a large canvas, three feet by six feet, which depicts in remarkable detail some of the high points of her life: actual covers of *Time, Life, Fortune,* and *The Architectural Forum,* magazines of

75

which her late husband, Henry Luce, was founder and publisher; the titles of one book *(Europe in the Spring)* and three plays *(Margin for Error, Kiss the Boys Good-bye,* and *The Women)* which she wrote; a "We Want Willkie" button from her political campaigns as well as a partial view of the U.S. Capitol where she served as a Congresswoman from Connecticut; an aerial view of Rockefeller Center and Saint Patrick's Cathedral; a globe and other objects representing her interest and involvement in national and international affairs. She made the canvas many years ago as a birthday present for her husband, taking two years to stitch it. It is now displayed under glass as a tabletop in the home of her stepson, Henry Luce III.

Tabletops are one of Mrs. Luce's favorite ways of displaying her needlepoint, and she has a number of them protected by glass in her home in Hawaii. She is also a great admirer of other people's quality needlework. She has a large collection of pillows by Maggie Lane, and she commissioned a set of dining-room chair seats, each featuring a different group of shells and coral native to the Hawaiian Islands.

Favorite needlepoint: Tabletop, three feet by six feet

Design: By Mrs. Luce

Canvas: No. 16 mono

Stitch: Basketweave

Russell Lynes

Wit and inventive style distinguish the needlepoint of Russell Lynes, not a surprising combination from an editor who straddles the art and literary worlds and a writer whose trenchant social observations have impaled us all in his three books, *Tastemakers*, *Snobs*, and *Highbrow, Lowbrow, Middlebrow*.

The qualities of wit and style are both abundantly manifest in Mr. Lynes' favorite needlepoint, a pair of hi-fi speaker covers that he considers among his most successful work. The two covers are trompe l'oeil deceivers involving the illusion of two shelves of books and other objects. They fit so believably into the Lynes living room bookcases that he has found to his chagrin that many guests don't ever discover they are needlepoint at all.

On close inspection you can see that the speaker covers are not only cleverly stitched but also tell a good deal about Mr. Lynes. Some of his published books share space with other, as yet unwritten, volumes slyly titled *Needlepoint, Trompe l'Oeil,*

Russell Lynes calls this view from his back window, mounted on a chair cushion, "The Garden of Eden." Note Adam and Eve, as well as the rooftop laundry and television antenna.

A geometric design with depth, created by Russell Lynes as he stitched it.

Using a kaleidoscope technique of his own, Russell Lynes creates three charming pillows.

Another geometric pillow design (left) by Russell Lynes, whose first piece of needlepoint was a blond nude (right) drawn for him by the cartoonist Steinberg.

A close-up of Russell Lynes'
trompe l'oeil needlepoint vest
(left). Note the convincing
eyeglasses and chain. At right is
a detail from one of a pair of
trompe l'oeil hi-fi speaker
covers.

and *R. L. Fecit 1968*. Perched atop a rendering of *Snobs* is a
needlepoint portrait of Cadwallader, the rat-hero of his satirical
novel of the same name, stitched from a little gray rubber rat
given Mr. Lynes by a friend. Next to a bound volume of *Harper's* magazine, of which he was managing editor for many
years and is still a contributing editor, is a silver mug holding
pencils, scissors, and a pipe, a duplicate of the real mug and its
contents on his writing desk. Above *The Domesticated Americans*
an owl swings on a hoop. A vermouth bottle, "which just happened to be around and fit," is wedged between a book whose
title is almost, but not really, legible, and a volume on whose
spine is Mr. Lynes' street address.

The possibilities of trompe l'oeil trickery first came to
mind shortly after Mr. Lynes took up needlepointing and, with
needle in hand and tongue in cheek, he designed a vest for

82

Detail from a second hi-fi speaker cover by Russell Lynes.

These details can be seen in full color in the insert following page 86.

himself. A stylish pinstripe, the vest is a masterpiece of illusion. A cigar, glasses, pencils, a ruler, theater tickets, and a dollar bill seem to peek out of four make-believe pockets, and a watch chain hangs realistically across the front. "The only trouble with the vest," says Mr. Lynes, "is that unless the temperature is below zero I never wear the thing. Too damn hot."

Another witty piece of descriptive needlepoint is a chair-seat cover called "The Garden of Eden." Actually, it is a view from the rear windows of his New York brownstone, encompassing the back of three neighboring buildings, fire escapes, television antennas, and a line of rooftop laundry. His own backyard Eden is also depicted, with the addition of Eve lolling on a bench, contemplating the lone apple in a tree, the serpent at her feet.

Needlepoint abounds in the Lynes home, along with stacks

of papers, walls of books, sketches, and paintings. Hanging over the dining room sideboard is his needlepoint version of his own painting of the Lynes summer home. "The painting is of summer. The needlepoint is early spring, don't you see? You cheat in your own favor," he points out with amusement. "Obviously, it's more trouble to stitch the full summer foliage."

The differences among the seasons caught Mr. Lynes' fancy, and he has stitched a set of four pillows representing Spring, Fall, Winter, and Summer, using a kaleidoscopic technique of his own invention. Marking the diagonals from corner to corner, he starts in the center of the canvas and improvises his way out to the edges, creating a fascinating, jewel-like patchwork of related forms.

Whereas most of his work is original, some treasured pieces have been designed by painter friends. His very first attempt at needlepoint, for instance, is a chair seat stitched from a drawing of a blond nude made for him by the cartoonist Steinberg. Hanging on a nearby wall is a tapestry from a Ben Shahn painting, the signatures stitched in Latin: "B. Shahn pinx, R. L. fecit." Mr. Lynes recalled, "Ben was absolutely fascinated—as any artist is—to see a technique he's used turned into another medium. You mix colors as in painting, but obviously, it's not exactly the same."

A particular favorite was derived from a peacock by Bernard Perlin, who has exhibited in the Whitney and other major museums. Perlin drew a colored crayon sketch that Mr. Lynes had photostated and enlarged to a thirty-inch square. In the enlargement, areas of solid color broke up into tiny dots of color (much like magnified newsprint), so he stitched it that way, borrowing the pointillist technique from painting. "There are no areas of solid color," explains Mr. Lynes. "All areas are made up of individual dots of color." To work pointil-listically, he carries one strand of yarn around the canvas, dis-tributing single stitches of color even though they may be widely separated. Then in the same manner, he fills in with similarly distributed dots of other colors, "scattering stitches at carefully controlled random." The result is a canvas with subtle iridescence and great depth. "I like to think I originated this needlepoint technique," he says with wry good humor, "but like everything you think you've done first, it was probably done elsewhere."

This fascination with colors is one of the particular plea-sures of needlepoint for Russell Lynes. "I use wool like paint," he says. "I like Persian wool, which has its own built-in bril-liance, and I try to enhance a canvas with a choice of colors." He uses a vast number of shades—for example, thirty or forty different greens are in his "Summer" pillow—and he works with them like an artist. "I use related greens, and yellows, and blues, and bounce colors against each other. Sometimes what makes a green come to life is a little red." He has a fairly clear idea of colors when he starts, but makes judgments as he goes along, "You know, like a painter. You think you need a little more yellow here." Like an artist getting the total effect of his work, he throws his needlepoint on the floor to look at it in lieu of standing back from an easel.

If Mr. Lynes sounds very much like a painter using needle and thread instead of brush and paint, it's no accident. "I'm enough of an art historian to see needlepoint as one way to cover blank space," he says. His interest in the medium prompted him to invite thirteen contemporary artists to design original needlepoint for *Art in America*, of which he was then a contributing editor. He himself gave up painting as soon as he stumbled on the delights of needlepoint through a grade-school daughter. "I was a Sunday painter, but at painting I was an amateur. At needlepoint, you can be a virtuoso!"

Favorite needlepoint: Two trompe l'oeil hi-fi speaker covers

Design: By Russell Lynes

Canvas: No. 10 penelope

Stitch: Basketweave

To get depth and iridescence, Russell Lynes stitched the peacock using an exacting pointillist technique he borrowed from painting and was the first to apply to needlepoint.

86

Russell Lynes, wearing his needlepoint vest, stands beside his trompe l'oeil hi-fi speaker cover, which successfully creates the illusion of a bookshelf that blends deceptively into the bookcase.

A second hi-fi speaker is concealed behind a similar needlepoint "bookshelf," which incorporates some real and some imagined titles by Russell Lynes. The rat is Cadwallader, hero of his satirical novel of the same name.

On the following two pages two remarkably accurate reproductions from the Louis Nizers' unique gallery of art masterpieces in needlepoint: "The Breasts with Red Flowers" by Gauguin (left) and "The Hindu Pose" by Matisse (right).

The head of a young girl was copied from Marie Laurencin by Louis Nizer and stitched by his wife, who incorporated both petit point (in the face) and gros point.

Animal motifs frequently turn up in Melanie Kahane's needlework, as in the skunk, owl, and crab designs shown here.

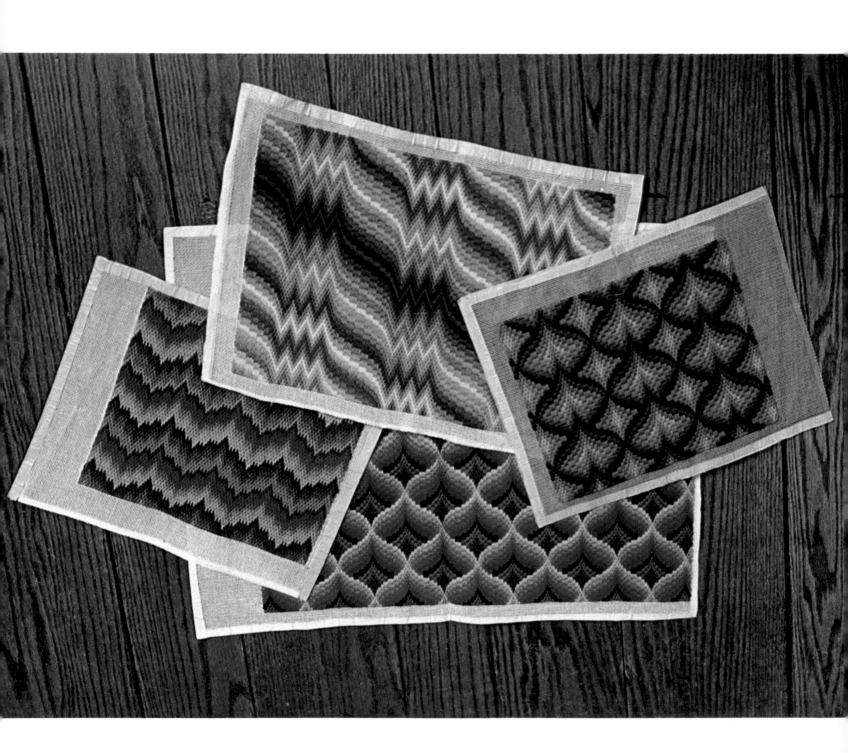

Meredith MacRae

As much a symbol of lively youth when she needlepoints as when she starred in *Hair*, Meredith MacRae quite naturally selects as her favorite kind of stitchery quick point, that fast-working stitch on large-mesh canvas that produces rapid results.

Miss MacRae was introduced to needlepoint by her best friend. "I had hooked a rug before, and so had Nancy. She went from rugs to needlepoint and suggested that I try it too. I bought a quick point canvas, which she thought was good for me to start on—a brown and yellow design."

Professional commitments for the busy young actress required much travel, which Miss MacRae put to good use. "I flew a great deal, and I found that planes are the perfect places to do needlepoint. You're sitting for hours with nothing to do, and when you get tired of reading, it's great to do needlework."

Enthusiasm for her new hobby prompted Miss MacRae to pick up a second quick point kit on a trip to New York—the

A group of unmounted bargello canvases that Betty Furness keeps on hand for gifts.

87

needlepoint that is her current favorite. It's a white pillow boldly patterned with kelly and olive-green checks. "The design caught my eye," she recalls, "and I thought it would be nice in our newly paneled den. I got most of it done on one really long flight."

Happily, the green-checked pillow turned into a family undertaking before it was finished. "My mother-in-law had been taking sewing lessons, and I thought I'd do the needlepoint part and she'd do the pillow part so she could practice her sewing. She was happy to block it and put it together for me." The green-backed pillow is permanently ensconced in the newly decorated den high in the hills above Los Angeles, where Miss MacRae and her husband, Greg Mulleavy, live in an eclectic environment of contemporary architecture and antique furnishings.

Her current needlepoint project is a third pillow, this one a tiny canvas with the message LOVE on it, designed for her by a friend. "I've done the LOVE, but not the background—it's so boring," said Miss MacRae, who likes her needlepoint quick and interesting.

Favorite needlepoint: Pillow with kelly and olive-green checks on white, twelve inches square

Design: Painted on canvas; from Bloomingdale's, New York

Canvas: No. 5 penelope

Stitch: Quick point

Meredith MacRae likes quick point canvas and geometric designs. Her favorite is at top right.

Dina Merrill

Dina Merrill's elegantly patrician exterior conceals remarkable enterprise and energy. A dedicated actress and president of her own cosmetics company, a division of Coty, she fills an active life with tennis, swimming, and golf, as well as career commitments.

Obviously not one to see time go to waste, Miss Merrill, who is married to actor Cliff Robertson, rekindled an interest in needlepoint a few years ago when she was expecting her youngest child. "My mother [Mrs. Marjorie Merriweather Post] taught me needlepoint when I was eight," she recalls. "Then I was busy with other things and forgot it completely. I began again when I was having Heather, and a needlepoint shop showed me the half cross and basketweave. I usually use a combination of the two stitches—one for background, the other for intricate designs."

The two stitches lend themselves to a wide variety of needlepoint projects, such as Miss Merrill's current one, a shell

Dina Merrill stitched this pair of tiger pillows for husband Cliff Robertson's study.

design. Like many enthusiasts, "My favorite needlepoint is usually the one I'm working on at the moment," she says. But pressed to single out one piece of work, her choice is a tiny suede-backed pillow copied from a small painting by a friend. "When I saw the original by Mrs. Julian Peabody, I loved it, and asked her to paint it for me on a needlepoint canvas." The piece traveled with Miss Merrill to Japan, where she made a movie called *The Walking Major*. While there she stitched on the set during lighting pauses.

"I needlepoint at odd moments, particularly when working and traveling," she explains. "Often when we have friends

92

Dina Merrill's favorite needlepoint (above) is based on the abstract painting (left) by her friend, Mrs. Julian Peabody.

over for dinner, I'll stitch while we talk. Cliff doesn't mind—in fact, he likes it."

Miss Merrill has also made needlepoint very much a family affair, passing the art down to her daughters in much the same way as she learned from her own mother. "I taught Steffi when she was eight, and she's now a good little worker. She made a pillow with a mouse and a larger mesh design with mushrooms. But then she was given a zebra that's too intricate, and that's thrown her. We'll probably do it as a joint project. I'll really teach Heather when she's older, but now, at the age of three, she likes to 'help' me put the needle in and out, or pull the

93

thread through—which delays me enormously, of course."

So far, Miss Merrill has concentrated on making pillows. She distributes them impartially between her large apartment high in New York City ("We sometimes look down on planes and clouds," she says of it) and a more informal country house in the Long Island dunes. For her husband's den in the city, she has stitched tiger pillows, which coordinate effectively with a chair covered in real zebra skin. At the beach house, two needlepoint butterfly pillows capture a country air.

Needlepoint other than her own is also displayed. In the New York living room, a large antique needlepoint rug sets the color scheme for a room filled with a fine collection of eighteenth-century furniture, scrimshaw, ivory ship models, and silver fish. A Portuguese needlepoint rug is used in the dining room, next to a handsome antique Queen Anne chair covered in bargello stitched by her mother. At the moment, Miss Merrill's own needlepoint plans are not quite so ambitious, although she is contemplating a piano bench cover.

Favorite needlepoint: Pillow with abstract design

Design: By Mrs. Julian Peabody, in yellow, orange, rust, red, blue, green, black, and white

Canvas: No. 10 mono

Stitch: Basketweave

Mary Tyler Moore

"This is my way of contributing to my home," says Mary Tyler Moore of her needlepoint. "I don't like to stitch gifts for other people. I'm very selfish about it because it takes a tremendous amount of time, and I want to put that time and effort into my home. You see, I don't cook and I don't entertain too much, so this is my way." When not actively involved in the popular "Mary Tyler Moore Show," she is usually in the modern beach house she describes as "a little French, a little English, a little modern, a lot of glass—just about everything I like, tied together with the advice of a decorator."

Among the needlepoint she has made for her home is the covering for an antique footstool given to her by her grandmother, stitched in deep purple with grape leaves and fruit clustered in the center. Also done in traditional style is a floral bellpull on a green background. A current project for her house, however, is more contemporary—a series of boldly colored pillows to line a window seat. "The subject is flowers," explains Miss Moore enthusiastically. "Each pillow is a different approach but in the same colors—vivid yellows and oranges and shocking pinks and purples and three shades of green—poison apple, forest, and kelly green. I think they'll be handsome," she says. Five of the pillows are already done, and five more are planned for a set of ten, all to be backed, lined, and tasseled alike.

The attractive needlepoint now displayed at Miss Moore's home was the serendipitous by-product of a hobby she took up for an entirely different reason. "I tried to give up smoking—and to keep my hands busy, I was initiated into needlepoint on the 'Dick Van Dyke Show' about 1963. I haven't yet been successful at giving up smoking—we'll make it some day—but I did become pretty good at needlepoint, so that's something."

Her first project, an evening bag, was not an easy one for a beginner. "I was working in dark brown, which, as you know, is very hard because you can't see the stitches very well. I almost went blind, and, in fact, that's how I had to wear glasses. But I just fell in love with it." She liked the bag so much that she later did a larger version of it, this time with a white background behind the cabbage rose and leaves.

Purses of all sizes and shapes are popular with Miss Moore, whose favorite needlepoint is a French coin purse she always carries with her. Yellow, gold, and black honeybees alight on the green background of the purse, which was designed with an extra gusset for additional room. "I work very quickly," says Miss Moore, "and the change purse only took me a week." It measures four by five inches, and is stitched in basketweave on No. 12 mono canvas, a finer mesh than the No. 10 canvas she usually uses.

Despite her denials, Miss Moore does indeed give away

needlepoint. "I did a coin purse and an eyeglass case for my mother that had orange and yellow ladybugs on it, similar to my coin purse." And she has made a belt for her husband. "I found a wonderful old brass buckle from a Civil War uniform," she says. "A needlepoint shop designed a camouflage pattern around it, in shades of brown, beige, and olive green. It's really great looking, and the first thing I've done just for him."

Perhaps the belt will still the objections her husband originally had to her needlepointing. "In the beginning, Grant kind of fought my needlepoint while we were watching television," she explains. "He's a TV producer, and he'd say, 'For heaven's sake, will you stop that and look what's going on. There's a good show here!' When I get involved in a project," she confesses, "I go at it furiously. With this set of pillows, for instance, I don't think I've read a newspaper in four months."

Most of her needlepoint is done at night because, as the star of her own television show, she's in every scene and, consequently, on the set all day working. "However," she explains, "One day a week—Thursday—is camera day and we do the scene once, then leave while the cameras block the scenes—and that's a time for me to needlepoint."

Despite her busy schedule and the shortness of time, Miss Moore keeps on producing and planning needlepoint projects. "One of the things I have had in the back of my mind forever," she says, "are the proverbial dining room chairs. But that's such a commitment. You can say, I'm going to do ten pillows and stop at seven. But once you start those dining room chairs, you've got to finish them. I think it might be flowers again, but in this case, one HUGE flower in the center of each chair— perhaps a giant daisy in one, a peony in another, a dandelion in a third—all with the same background. But unless you had

Mary Tyler Moore's favorite is a roomy French coin purse with honey bees.

some elves hidden somewhere to do the background stitches for you . . ." her voice trails off in awe at the enormity of her scheme.

How, one wonders, can a woman with a demanding career even contemplate stitching a set of dining room chairs? Miss Moore offers the answer herself. "There's something very relaxing about needlepoint for me. I guess it's the same satisfaction that one gets from sculpting or painting in that it's an art form, with a degree of self-expression—a combination of art and craft. And it's lasting—I love that—and nothing is ever going to hurt it. Most important, it's what I give to my home."

Favorite needlepoint: French coin purse with bee design

Design: By Jebba, Inc., Los Angeles, California, in gold, yellow, and black on green background

Canvas: No. 12 mono

Stitch: Basketweave

98

Mr. & Mrs. Louis Nizer

"It's a museum gallery," says Mrs. Louis Nizer proudly of the collection of art masterpieces stitched in needlepoint and embedded in the dining room walls of her New York penthouse. The unusual gallery is the joint creation of Louis Nizer, the well-known lawyer, and his wife, who both enjoy art in many forms. Their unique personal art collection, ranging from Marie Laurencin to Noel Coward, covers walls in every room, and includes a great many signed Louis Nizer.

The dining gallery boasts eight art masterpieces translated into needlepoint: the delicate face of a young girl, after Marie Laurencin; a spare composition of a skull and white roses, from Georgia O'Keefe; a pastel composition incorporating two ladies on horseback and a ballet dancer, derived from a Marie Laurencin painting hanging in the Nizers' own living room; two Polynesian women from a Gauguin work called "The Breasts with Red Flowers"; "Irises in a Vase," from Van Gogh; "Two Horses," from de Chirico; "The Hindu Pose," from Matisse, resembling one of the artist's odalisques; and a primitive design with monkeys and oranges in a forest, from Henri Rousseau.

The needlepoint pictures are not in uniform sizes or shapes, but vary from small rectangular paintings with needlepoint "mats," as the Gauguin, Matisse, and de Chirico are handled, to larger free-form pieces where the subject matter virtually comes off the edge of the canvas. The needlepoint "paintings" flank the wrought iron gates to the room and line both long walls.

The stitched masterpieces were not always mounted on the walls, but originally were made as seat covers for the dining room chairs. About ten years ago when the Nizers were redecorating their apartment, they thought of a needlepoint gallery, feeling the stitched reproductions would be more effective on the walls and enjoyed by more people. "Most guests get a kick out of recognizing them all," reports Mrs. Nizer. Each piece of needlepoint was embedded in a large plywood panel that was mounted on the dining room walls, then covered with a soft green fabric closely resembling the basketweave stitch.

Committing art works to needlepoint is a fascinating process that begins when Mrs. Nizer chooses the paintings and buys reproductions of them. Then, using the reproduction as a model, Mr. Nizer draws each picture freehand on a needlepoint canvas, a little at a time. "You can never draw the whole painting on the canvas at once," he explains. "Look at the ones made that way—any discerning eye would see the difference. You build it up an eighth of an inch at a time."

Reproducing the colors and finding the right shades of yarn are two of the difficulties of transposing a piece of art to another medium. "You can't duplicate the colors exactly," says Mr. Nizer, "but you can achieve a similar relationship of colors.

Mr. and Mrs. Louis Nizer at home.

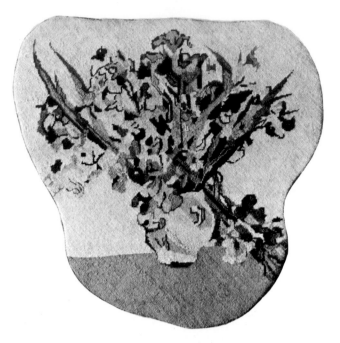

Van Gogh's "Irises in a Vase" reproduced by the Louis Nizers.

"Two Horses" by de Chirico, faithfully translated into needlepoint by Mr. and Mrs. Louis Nizer.

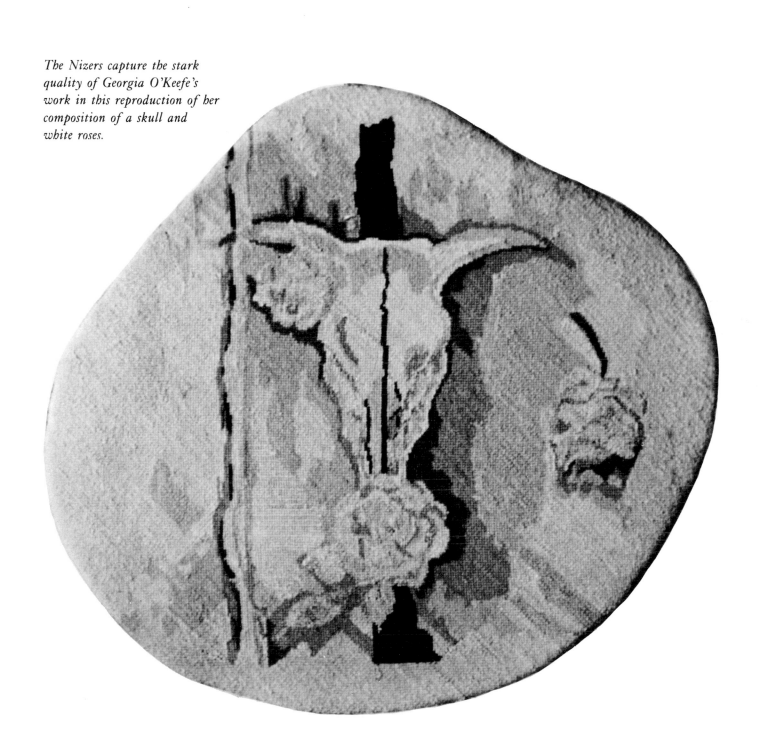

The Nizers capture the stark quality of Georgia O'Keefe's work in this reproduction of her composition of a skull and white roses.

A primitive design of monkeys and oranges in a forest, from an Henri Rousseau painting, as stitched by Mr. and Mrs. Louis Nizer.

Details from one of the monkeys from the Rousseau design.

As an amateur painter, I have learned that colors are constantly changing, that areas are composed of many colors. A face is never flesh colored, for instance; it reflects the surroundings, the light. Painting is like writing—it's observation," observes Mr. Nizer who is both a painter and a writer.

Mr. Nizer draws on penelope canvas, which Mrs. Nizer prefers to mono, using No. 10 mesh and sometimes even as fine a canvas as No. 14 mesh. She splits the double weave for details. Through these intricate areas, Mr. Nizer sits with his wife as she works. "I really have to have him watch me," says Mrs. Nizer, adding with fond admiration, "He has much more patience than I have about it."

"Patience" is not the word Mr. Nizer uses to describe his intimate involvement with the needlepoint project. "I'm inclined to be a perfectionist," he acknowledges, "and everything I do must be done well. I wouldn't allow a line that's wrong."

Contemplating the unique museum that took them over fifteen years to produce, the Nizers discuss their favorites among them. "I'm torn between the Rousseau and the Gauguin," says Mrs. Nizer. After hesitating a moment, Mr. Nizer picks the Gauguin, "—probably because it was the most difficult to draw. It was hard to get depth and roundness in the two figures." While Mr. Nizer appraises the gallery with an artist's eye, Mrs. Nizer is keenly conscious of the stitching involved. "The Georgia O'Keefe was the easiest to do, because it has so many broad areas of color. But only a fool would do some of them," she says ruefully. "I didn't know enough about it when we started to know how difficult it would be."

Less difficult but also satisfying was another collaborative effort, a pillow Mr. Nizer designed and drew, listing his early books: *Thinking on Your Feet*, *What To Do With Germany*, *New*

Courts of Industry, and *Between You and Me*. Mrs. Nizer stitched not only the title design but the back of the pillow as well, creating, in effect, a needlepoint backing that looks like fabric. She is currently working on a companion pillow that lists his most recent books, *My Life in Court* and *The Jury Returns*.

What about Mr. Nizer's many paintings that grace the walls of both his home and office? Is there any thought of reproducing them in needlepoint? "I could probably do one of his paintings," says Mrs. Nizer, considering his rendition of a large vase of flowers. "Don't tell him I said so," she confides privately, "but I'd rather do a masterpiece."

Doubtless, her remark would please Mr. Nizer who believes, "The idea is to have masterpieces—but that you did yourself. There's no point in painting a copy. What's important is that you have translated them into a different and difficult medium like needlepoint."

Favorite needlepoint: Eight art masterpieces, after Gauguin, Matisse, Van Gogh, de Chirico, O'Keefe, Rousseau, and two Laurencins.

Design: Adapted by Louis Nizer

Canvas: Penelope Nos. 10 and 14

Stitch: Basketweave

Janis Paige

"Your favorite, I guess, is always the first thing you did," Janis Paige observes thoughtfully, looking back over the diverse pieces of needlepoint she has stitched in the past few years. Her first was actually two—a pair of bench cushions she made for her very large, old parlor grand. One cushion has a leopard in the center surrounded by fuchsia, blue, and orange stripes. The other is bordered in a brown and black leopard print. "Instead of using one large piano bench," Miss Paige explains, "I use two smaller Empire seats, each two and a half feet long and eighteen inches wide. "I love those cushions. They're my favorite because they're close to me."

"I was in a musical in New York called *Here's Love*," she recalls, "and found myself very tense. One day I saw an offer for some needlepoint kits filled with leopard designs and brilliant colors. I'm especially fond of anything to do with leopards, so I sent for three of the kits. I had never done needlepoint in my life. I just read the diagrams and began."

The kits were intended as pillows, but Miss Paige simply adapted them to her needs. "One of them had an empty space," she remembers, "so I just left out part of the design and did my own. I wanted to incorporate my own ideas. One has my wedding date on it, and the other has the name of my puppy, Jody. I redrew some of the design, not knowing exactly what I was doing, but I loved it and I wanted to do something that was personal for the house."

The two bench covers took Miss Paige two to three months to stitch. "I could only work on them intermittently," she explains. "I did them in my dressing room before the show at night because I always get to the theater terribly early and I like the quiet when no one's around. And when I'm in New York, I'm a real night owl, so I'd get home after the show, have my dinner, and do some more needlepoint."

The cushions have given Miss Paige continued pleasure. "I'm really very proud of them," she says. "They didn't quite fit the benches, but I've done them with velvet bindings and sides, so they're quite effective in the house." In the large, walnut-paneled living room, they sit before the old parlor grand. "It's a very old, very carved, motion-picture piano," Miss Paige says, "and I've had it restored." Underneath the piano, crouching on the white tile floor, is Miss Paige's collection of leopard cats. "I've loved leopards all my life," she says. "I've studied them, and have books on them, and my husband always buys me leopards whenever he sees an odd one."

Miss Paige's passion for leopards extends to other pieces of needlepoint as well. She is currently working on a vest designed with two leopard cubs, one on his back with his feet in the air, the other sitting among daisies and leaves and all kinds of flowers. "It's on a black background, which is killing me," she says. "It's murder to work on because it's sixteen mesh canvas, and it just doesn't go fast enough for me."

Like the two piano benches, most of Miss Paige's needlepoint has personal meaning for her. Her near-favorite piece, for instance, is a pair of slippers she stitched for her husband, a writer, composer, and publisher. "When we went to Rio," she recalls, "his first hit song was 'A Dozen Yellow Roses,' so I designed needlepoint slippers with a yellow rose on each toe—and had a terrible time doing it," she adds.

Even her tray straps are special. "I don't think anyone else has them," she says proudly of the malachite design drawn for her by her good friend and needlepoint expert Lou Gartner. "He did them for me as an opening night present, then he brought me a beautiful set of trays from Italy to use with them."

Her gifts, too, receive an individual touch to make them really special for the lucky recipients. "I try to put something personal in the pillows I make for people," she says. "For friends of mine in New York who were married a few years ago I drew a great big old-fashioned heart on a zebra background, with their names and the wedding date on it. They loved it."

Where, with stage, film, and television commitments, does a busy actress find time to produce so much needlepoint? "I love it," Miss Paige says emphatically. "I find it terribly relaxing. I find that I can do needlepoint and other things at the same time. For instance, if I'm learning a script or a score—like *Applause*, which I just did in South Africa—I learn the lyrics and the music while I needlepoint. I've trained my mind to do it," she says proudly, "so I can accomplish two things at one time!"

110

Favorite needlepoint: Two piano benches with leopard themes

Design: Adapted by Miss Paige from kits

Canvas: No. 10 penelope

Stitch: Half cross

Close-up of the gold presidential seal stitched into a pair of slippers made as a gift for President Lyndon B. Johnson by Mollie Parnis. The slippers can be seen in full color in the insert following page 22.

Mollie Parnis

Behind the busy Mollie Parnis Seventh Avenue showroom, where the rich and famous choose their clothes, is a private retreat. Here, the well-known designer looks wryly at a handsome pair of needlepoint slippers she has made as a birthday present for a friend. Gold initials were neatly centered on a black background to form the throat of the leather bedroom shoes, but the recipient had apologetically returned them because the size was slightly wrong.

"I don't think he realizes these cost fifty dollars to finish," the forthright Miss Parnis remarks ruefully.

Another pair of Parnis slippers were received more enthusiastically—this time by a President of the United States. Stitched for Lyndon Johnson as a surprise Christmas gift in 1967, the black slippers with gold presidential seal are Miss Parnis's all-time favorite needlepoint project. That the former President was enormously pleased with her stitchery is shown by the place of honor given the slippers in the Lyndon B. Johnson Library.

Miss Parnis had met Mrs. Johnson while designing clothes for the former First Lady, and a warm friendship developed that soon included the whole Johnson family. "While planning the slippers, I consulted the President's secretary for his size," Miss Parnis recalls, as she fingers the circular gold pendant with the presidential seal that was a gift to her from Mr. Johnson. "I don't remember the size now, but they were big. He's a big man." The design for the needlepoint seal was copied, not from her pendant, but from a seal readily available to the public. Miss Parnis relied on shades of yellows and golds to portray the seal, adding no gilt.

Making needlepoint that she can give away is one of the satisfactions Miss Parnis gets from stitchery. Another gift—a pillow for Kirk Douglas—was inspired by his greeting to his wife on coming home tired from work: "The king is home. I want a little attention, please." Miss Parnis asked her workroom to design a "seal" incorporating the masks of tragedy and comedy and the initials of Kirk Douglas, all surmounted with a kingly crown. For her son, she has made a Mondrian-design pillow and a monogrammed pillow, and then, after his plea, "No more pillows," a pair of red slippers with his initials in navy blue.

Such men's slippers are a favorite gift with Miss Parnis, and she has stitched and presented them, either in solid black or red, to more than twenty friends. (Female friends, however, are out of luck. "I tried to make a pair of lady's slippers, but they just didn't turn out well," she says.) Except for the presidential seal, all the bedroom slippers are stitched with the initials of the recipient across the throat of the slipper, for Miss Parnis likes to personalize her gifts.

Despite the lavish flow of presents, needlepoint doesn't have a consistent claim on Miss Parnis's attention. "I'll get carried away and work on something for a month or six weeks, then not touch it again for six months," she says. "Needlepoint to me is an extra dimension. If I get hooked on a project, I find this the most wonderful way to relax. I do it really to keep busy," she continues enthusiastically. "Like most busy people, I feel guilty about wasting time, and the biggest waster of time, in my opinion, is television. So I needlepoint when I watch it." Miss Parnis also does a great deal of stitching on planes, and invariably takes along a canvas to work on vacation. "But that doesn't mean I always get to it," she admits.

Needlepoint as a pastime, and fashion as a business, have no point of contact for Miss Parnis, who dismisses needlepoint handbags and accessories as being "too artsy-craftsy." She hastens to add, "I don't mean someone couldn't do something marvelous with it, but I really don't think it belongs."

She does think that needlepoint belongs in a home—within limits. In her own duplex apartment, she has half a dozen pillows plumped up on the bed in the guest room, and says flatly, "That's enough pillows." She has considered a needlepoint rug, but isn't yet willing to tackle such an ambitious project, saying, "I don't do it well enough to start a rug, and I envy anyone who can carry through. So I always work on small pieces like the slippers and pillows that don't have too much design."

Currently, Miss Parnis is working on a pillow she designed herself, based on a Persian scarf from her own collection. It has more shading and detail than she is accustomed to. "I think I bit off more than I can chew," she frankly admits. "It was much

easier to design than to stitch. I really prefer simple motifs—
the pieces that have given me the most satisfaction to make are
those slippers."

Favorite needlepoint: Bedroom slippers with presidential seal

Design: Copied from a presidential seal and painted on the
canvas

Canvas: No. 12 mono

Stitch: Basketweave

Roberta Peters

"A right-handed stitcher will tell you it's easy, but when you get to the end of the line . . ." Roberta Peters' soprano voice trails off, with the resignation of a leftie trying to learn a new handicraft in a world of right-handed instructors. "I kept having trouble at the end of the row, not knowing whether to turn it upside down or not," explains the Metropolitan Opera star. After frustrating bouts with the needle and much ripping out of stitches, she eventually mastered one stitch—the continental—and, pleased with her success and her new hobby, says proudly, "Now I know what I'm doing."

With the hard-won victory in hand, she describes her first —and favorite—needlepoint project, a small pillow with a pink and blue bird set against a stylized green landscape and puffy white clouds in a blue sky. "The bird is so pretty—so light and gay," Miss Peters says approvingly. "I love it for that reason. I don't care for birds flying around, but I have some china birds in a collection, and I think they're pretty on canvas."

Actually, the little blue bird did fly around, for Miss Peters stitched it mainly while traveling on planes. "Needlepoint is easy to take on the plane," she says. "I like to do it there, and sometimes in the evening when we're watching television. But mostly I save it for when I'm on trips, because at home I have a million things to do."

Unlike many stage and screen actresses who stitch large swatches of needlepoint in their dressing rooms, Miss Peters says emphatically, "I never do it backstage—my mind is elsewhere. And I don't have enough time, with rehearsals and costume fittings." But even restricting her needlepoint mainly to traveling, Miss Peters finds ample time to pursue her new hobby. Her career frequently takes her around the world, from the Metropolitan Opera House in New York to the Vienna State Opera, from concert stages at the new Kennedy Center in Washington to Israel, where she makes frequent appearances, once even singing to the Israeli troops during the Six-Day War.

The bluebird canvas was a gift from a friend, a timely one, she acknowledges. "I was ready for needlepoint and probably would have started even if no one had given me a canvas." The finished pillow, backed in light blue velvet, may also be a gift —to fellow opera artist, Jan Peerce. "Many years ago he made a record of 'The Bluebird of Happiness,' which turned into a best seller, so I think I may save this to give him for a birthday or anniversary."

Until that time the pillow nestles in a corner of a roomy blue leather couch in "The Blue Room," the comfortable library where Miss Peters and her husband, Bertram Fields, spend most of their free evenings, surrounded by a wall of books and contemporary art, including one of the paintings

Detail from Roberta Peters'
favorite needlepoint, a bluebird
of happiness pillow. The entire
pillow can be seen in full color
in the insert following page 22.

Marc Chagall did for a stage setting for the Metropolitan Opera production of *The Magic Flute*. A second canvas (also a gift) that she's working on is destined for the same room. It has a traditional, prestitched floral arrangement in the center, and Miss Peters chose a blue background. "It's not as much fun to do just the background," she remarks. "I like to do all the design myself."

119

While filling in the background of her floral piece, Miss Peters is looking forward with a cautious eye to future projects. "I'm not planning a big needlepoint project. I'm not too adventurous yet," she says. "I only know one stitch (the continental). I have not been experimental, and I don't care to be at this point. Somebody told me about bargello, but I don't think I'm ready for it yet." Nor does Miss Peters want to do anything related to a role in a favorite opera, such as *Don Giovanni*, *The Marriage of Figaro*, *The Magic Flute*, or *Rigoletto*. "I think," she muses, "I'll do one for my eleven-year-old son, perhaps boats. He wants one for his room."

Still conscious of being a novice stitcher, and sympathetic to other lefties who may encounter difficulties, Miss Peters offers this advice: "Get a good teacher—someone who *really* knows how to do it left-handed."

Favorite needlepoint: Blue Heaven pillow, nine by seven inches

Design: By Jebba, Inc., Los Angeles, California

Canvas: No. 12 mono

Stitch: Continental

Lyn Revson

Selecting colors for needlepoint to go in a husband's office may pose a dilemma for anyone. But imagine if the husband were Charles Revson, head of Revlon and a man so noted for his precise color judgment that it is said he can unerringly pick from 100 lipsticks the single shade destined for success!

Lyn Revson's simple solution is to let Charles choose. "He has a terrific color sense!" she says appreciatively. She then devotes her own considerable energies to turning out beautifully stitched canvases in startling quantity. Her husband is so pleased with the results that he is inclined to snatch them up as soon as completed to go on permanent display in his office. "He has most of my needlepoint there," she explains. "For instance, I was making a rug for a bathroom. It would have been very chic, but he loved it so much that it's now in front of his desk."

Lyn Revson obviously delights in delighting her husband, saying candidly of needlepoint in general, "He likes it—that's

Lyn Revson's favorite is taken from a frequent expression of her husband Charles's. She has stitched the same design in three different colors for his Revlon office.

why I do it. He considers it creative." Unlike some husbands who dislike the distraction of a wife immersed in stitchery, he enjoys being with her when she's at work. "We sit here," she gestures around a comfortable room in the Revsons' triplex penthouse, "and I work while we watch television. He's delighted to see me start stitching—it gives him an opportunity to get on the phone."

During these occasional evenings at home, or in the late afternoons when she's waiting for her husband, Lyn Revson has produced an incredible amount of needlework, all the more overwhelming when you consider that she often works with

122

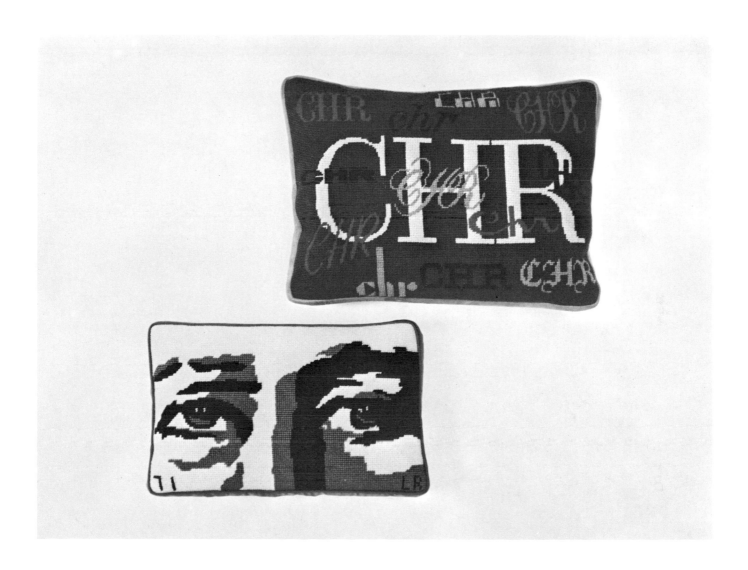

Two pillows—one featuring her husband's monogram, the other a portrait of his eyes and eyebrows—by Lyn Revson.

silk thread on tiny mesh canvas, and has only been seriously stitching for seven years. "I sometimes work when traveling, but I don't do it much on our boat, although I thought I would," she says. "And I sometimes stop to let my fingernails grow. Working on coarse rug canvas wears them straight across." But then she adds thoughtfully, "Sometimes I don't take anything at all with me and then I'm sorry." Waiting and ready to go at a moment's notice are multiple needlepoint projects, each in its Hermes bag. Looking closely at one petit point canvas, you can see a number of threaded needles in work simultaneously—perhaps one secret of her productivity.

Creatures of the sea and sky, based on Maggie Lane designs, meet in this handsome rug stitched by Lyn Revson. The entire rug can be seen in full color in the insert following page 22.

Possibly because her work is apt to catch her husband's eye and end up in his office, Mrs. Revson says, "I never make a piece of needlepoint for any particular place. I just make it." And despite the flow of finished work to Mr. Revson's office, she still has many samples at home. A pair of petit point floral pillows and a pair of Chinese scenes enliven a sumptuous wood-paneled salon. Two small chairs covered with needlepoint stand in a hall, and an apricot and white hall rug welcomes a visitor to her comfortable apricot and white sitting room. Partially finished is an unusual eleven-piece rug. Its three long, elegantly simple center strips are worked primarily in beige and framed with eight charming and colorful animal scenes, the whole so enormous that once it is joined together it will probably remain in the family room for which it is intended.

In addition to the needlepoint that her husband adopts, Mrs. Revson makes a great many pieces specifically as gifts for him. "I did a small rectangular pillow showing only a pair of eyes and eyebrows. My husband has eyes that are really outstanding, and this little canvas reminded me of him. Then I did "CHR" as a centered monogram, surrounded by many sets of his initials in script, slanting, printing, all different sizes and styles." Another gift for him currently in work is a delicate and beautiful Chinese figure which she describes as "a man of long life. The peach in his hand and oriental symbols around the border all symbolize long life," she explains. It, too, is in petit point, and the border an exacting job of counting threads. "I did one entire margin, then discovered it was one stitch off. I'm sure no one would notice, but I'm a perfectionist, so I ripped it all out. I ripped and ripped on that piece."

The Revsons also have a fondness for committing amusing mottoes and sayings to canvas, some of which make their way straight from Mr. Revson's conversation. For instance, two framed mottoes adorn his office dining room: "Business is Business and Friendship is Friendship," a favorite Revson quote, and "Oh Lord Give Me a Bastard With Talent." (Mrs. Revson is now stitching the companion piece in answer to the latter: "Oh Lord I Hope My Prayers Are Answered.") In his office sitting room is a pillow stitched in beige and a range of lipstick reds with the words, "In My Considered Opinion." "That's a phrase," confides Mrs. Revson, "with which my husband starts practically every sentence. But if I had to choose one favorite, it would be a frequent expression of his: 'Nobody Loves a Smart Ass.' Oh, how he loves that motto! He had me make three or four pillows with it in different colors, one right after another—all for his office."

Favorite needlepoint: "Nobody Loves a Smart Ass," 11 inches by 13 inches

Design: By Lyn Revson

Canvas: No. 10 mono

Stitch: Basketweave

Dorothy Rodgers

In some circles, Dorothy Rodgers is nearly as well known for her needlepoint as her husband, Richard Rodgers, is for his musicals. Her laurels don't rest with her favorite hobby, however. Mrs. Rodgers is that *rara avis*, a famous man's wife who has successfully managed her own independent achievements —as decorator, inventor, and author. Her latest book, *A Word to the Wives*, written with her daughter Mary, spawned a joint monthly column in *McCall's* magazine. And with all her other accomplishments, Dorothy Rodgers is also celebrated as a creative hostess and homemaker.

In the Rodgers' New York apartment, needlepoint is an unobtrusive, although integral, part of the décor, which mixes eighteenth-century antique furniture with collections of miniature chests and Battersea enamel, photographs of family and friends, a profusion of flowers, and a large collection of sculpture and paintings that ranges from pre-Columbian figures to Jackson Pollock oils. Needlepoint pillows of all sizes and shapes

127

are tucked comfortably into chairs. Rugs (among them a prize winner from a Bucks County fair) are stitched in shades and shapes reflecting their location. In her husband's study, a bargello-covered cornice effectively frames the room's windows, and in his bedroom, the headboard and footboard of his Empire sleigh bed are upholstered with needlepoint panels stitched to match the yellow bedspread.

One rug in which Mrs. Rodgers obviously takes great pride was a joint venture with her daughter Linda, planned for Linda's bedroom. Since the bed would cover much of the rug, Mrs. Rodgers sensibly proposed a wide border of needlepoint, designed to match the Porthault linens. "There was no point in making the whole rug of needlepoint," says Mrs. Rodgers practically, "since most of it would be hidden by the bed." Together she and Linda stitched four long strips that were attached to and frame the white rug.

Not all of Mrs. Rodgers' needlepoint is on display. Other completed projects, including a number of rugs, are still kept in closets, as are the bargello bedroom slippers for her husband and sons-in-law, and a bargello briefcase and matching pocketbook for herself.

Although Mrs. Rodgers is delighted to share her needlepoint with the family, she rarely stitches for others. "I don't believe in giving needlepoint as a gift, any more than I would a painting, because taste is so personal. After all," she continues with a special sensitivity, "it's my hobby, and just because I've enjoyed making something, why should someone else have to use it? At most, gifts should be something tiny like an eyeglass case."

Where, one wonders, is the time in which to fill so many canvases with wool? "I needlepoint while watching television," is Mrs. Rodgers' partial explanation, "and I never miss a murder." She is a rapid worker, and also plies her needle when on the road with her husband's shows, and during other travels, or when talking with friends. It's easy to suspect that she is unusually well organized, wasting neither minutes nor stitches.

Needlepoint has been a hobby of Mrs. Rodgers' since her childhood, when she remembers watching her governess make beaded bags, and she decided to apply beading to finished needlepoint, a technique she has used on needlepoint pillows. To improve her facility she took a course at the Royal School of Needlework in London. "I really went to learn crewel," she says, "but I found it was not for me. You have to make a choice every time you make a stitch. So I learned some different needlepoint stitches instead."

Many of her early needlepoint pieces were traditional, often flowered, and always stitched from painted canvases. In recent years, however, she has discovered the delights of working out original designs. She usually plans them on graph paper, then transfers them to canvas with an indelible marker, outlining the major forms and then filling in freehand, judging the shading and placement of colors as she stitches. "It's much more satisfying to work on your own designs," she says. "It also cuts down greatly on the cost, since all I buy is canvas and wool. That still leaves the cost of mounting the needlepoint, of course, but you can block your own pillows or rugs if you know how and have the room."

As Mrs. Rodgers turned away from painted canvases, her work has progressed from intricate floral pieces to geometric shapes and experiments with shading colors. "Sometimes I blend strands of wool. For instance, one square of darkest color, the second square substituting a lighter strand for one of the

dark strands, the third square using still lighter strands blended together, and so on. Most of my current projects have been very three-dimensional, like the geometric design in shades of pink that I'm working on now. I did so many traditional things that I got bored with them."

In this contemporary trend is Mrs. Rodgers' favorite needlepoint, a large pillow based on an op art painting—a construction of cubes in seemingly shifting perspectives—by Victor Vasarely. Using graph paper, she adapted it from a small photograph she saw in a news magazine, changing the colors, simplifying the interior form of the figure, and quadrupling the size in the photograph. When her design was worked out, she drew the one large form on canvas with an indelible marker and worked the shading as she stitched, judging by eye where the subtle gradations changed from white through soft grays to charcoal. "I had no way of knowing if it was going to work," she says. "I'd stitch a while, then put the canvas across the room to let the values emerge." The result is a fascinating geometric puzzle with the depth and movement of a crystal prism. The central figure is stitched in basketweave, and the background is in mosaic stitch, which Mrs. Rodgers often uses because it goes quickly.

The needlepoint is centered on one side of a box pillow, framed with slender self-welting, and bordered by the same raw silk in which the pillow is finished. It shares the sofa in her husband's brown and beige study with a pillow made for the Rodgers by Mary Martin, which catches the hands of Richard Rodgers composing "Bali Ha'i" for *South Pacific*.

Over the years Mrs. Rodgers has shared her enthusiasm for needlework with many friends, including Mrs. Robert Sherwood, wife of the late dramatist, and Mrs. Oscar Hammerstein,

The subtle relationships of color and form in a Vasarely op art painting were adapted to needlepoint by Dorothy Rodgers in this handsome pillow.

131

who had been an attentive observer as they traveled on the road with Rodgers and Hammerstein productions. Mrs. Rodgers reminisces about two of her earliest needlepoint projects, tiny gray silk butterfly pillows. "Mary Martin and Dick Halliday came to dinner one night when I was working on them. They were just learning to needlepoint, so Dick did one of the small butterflies."

For beginners not lucky enough to work with her personally, Mrs. Rodgers offers some general suggestions:

Start with something small, such as an eyeglass case or a small pillow, and be prepared to throw it away as a learning piece when finished.

Learn the basketweave stitch from the beginning. "It's easy to learn if you've never stitched before."

Try bargello work and the Gobelin stitch, both are excellent for novices.

Favorite needlepoint: Adaptation of "Gestalt-Sang" by Victor Vasarely

Design: By Mrs. Rodgers in tones of white, beige, and charcoal on a brown background

Canvas: No. 14 mono

Stitches: Basketweave for central figure; mosaic for background

Aline Saarinen

Art critic and historian, television journalist, and now Chief of NBC News' Paris Bureau, Aline Saarinen has spent her life among creative and articulate people. Not surprisingly, she enjoys needlepoint most when it is original and her own. "I really don't like buying a pattern," she says. "It's less fun than the things you do yourself."

"My favorite needlepoint? As architects often say, it's the project I'm working on now—or even the next one."

Her current and therefore favorite project is a large one, a rug of fifteen individual segments inspired by Dahomey legends and planned as a Christmas gift for her son and daughter-in-law, Donald and Pingree Louchheim, who closely collaborated on the project. The Louchheims were living in Africa when they bought a native appliqué depicting monsters and fish, each symbol recalling the word or deed of a Dahomey king. Pingree, charmed by the legend, adapted it for needlepoint and sent it to Mrs. Saarinen, who had been wanting to make them a rug.

"Pingree is very talented," says Mrs. Saarinen with obvious pride. "She made separate drawings of the segments so I would have stitching checkpoints, and she painted the canvas." A certain amount of revision and editing took place before all the figures got final approval. "Originally, three symbols she drew were not animals, although they were all part of the legend. I thought it should all be animals, so I said to Ping, when you transfer something from one medium to another, you change its character, obviously. Let's make it *based* on the legend. Ping said, 'I'll think primitive.' And she drew a marvelous snake and two lizards."

The strong primary colors of the rug—red, blue, and yellow on a black background—are almost the national colors of Dahomey. "She has constructed this thing very well," Mrs. Saarinen comments approvingly. "The relationship of the col-

Drawings for two sections of Aline Saarinen's favorite rug, inspired by Dahomey legends. The animals were drawn by her daughter-in-law, Pingree Louchheim.

134

ors is extremely subtle. When you try shifting the squares around, you can see it."

Each twelve-inch square of the rug took about a month to stitch. Finished squares, keyed to their position in the rug, were kept in well-organized storage, ready to be assembled with a border. Mrs. Saarinen, who needlepoints when traveling, remembers, "I started that yellow fish on the way to film 'The Prado' [a television art special] in Madrid." She also works while watching television. "I have to watch a lot of TV, and with big stitches, you can do needlepoint almost by Braille." The rug, like almost everything else Mrs. Saarinen stitches, is on No. 10 canvas because, as she says, "It goes fast and I'm impatient."

Making the rug took well over a year, and, Mrs. Saarinen recalls, "Everybody asked if I don't feel badly about people walking on it after so much work. Not at all. I think that's sort of the fun—the sense that through the ages these things change and happen. I'm even told that needlepoint will outlast us. But Donald and Ping thought they'd hang it on the wall anyway for a while."

Obviously, Mrs. Saarinen enjoys making needlepoint gifts for her family. One sentimental favorite is a long, thin giraffe, originally designed as a bell pull. "I added inch marks along the side to measure the heights of the three grandchildren," she explains, "and stitched 'Jess,' 'Jeff,' and 'Joe,' to show how tall each child was when the family left Paris in July of 1969. Already these kids have such fun because they go back and see how little they were at the time."

An earlier project was a set of needlepoint seats for six Eames dining chairs. The cross-and-square pattern was suggested by Mrs. Saarinen's brother, in accordance with the views on needlepoint design of Eero Saarinen, the world famous architect. "My late husband had a period when he felt it was wrong for the medium to do curves—he was a purist about that," Mrs. Saarinen explains. "I once made him a pair of needlepoint slippers he had designed in geometrics."

The colors for the dining chair seats—greens, tans, and fuschia "hot spots"—were derived from a prized Paul Klee painting. "There was no total plan for the chairs," says Mrs. Saarinen. "I just improvised as I made them. They are alike, but not identical. I was making a film in Paris while working on one, and I remember being very angry with someone—and that seat has a much bigger hot spot."

Favorite needlepoint: Rug based on a Dahomey legend. Made in fifteen sections, each twelve inches square

Design: Adapted by Mrs. Donald Louchheim and Mrs. Saarinen; in red, blue, yellow on a black background

Canvas: No. 10 mono

Stitch: Basketweave

U. S. Cabinet Wives

Although effervescent Martha Mitchell instigated a needlepoint project for Nixon administration Cabinet wives, she didn't get to take a stitch herself. "I used to needlepoint, but I don't have time anymore," she drawls. "I'm usually working— even when I'm on the phone."

The idea of asking the wives of the original Cabinet members—as well as Mrs. Nixon and Mrs. Agnew—to make their husbands' seals of office for Blair House occurred to Mrs. Mitchell because, she remembers, "We were looking for a project that would be lasting." A needlepoint designer, Rosetta Larsen, transferred the official seals to canvas after researching them in the public library. "Of course, you have to adapt sometimes because of the square meshes of the canvas," Miss Larsen explained. "For instance, the President's stars are not really stars, but impressions of stars."

The needlepoint project was launched at a luncheon, and each wife was presented with a painted canvas of her husband's seal and the necessary yarns: Persian wools in beige for all backgrounds, appropriate colors for the seals, and silk thread for highlighting eagle feathers and gold stars. In each kit enough of the design was worked to get the women started.

Even with this beginning boost, a few of the wives were too busy to do their own work. Mrs. Nixon turned the presidential seal over to her social secretary, and a Washington newspaperwoman completed the Attorney General's seal for Mrs. Mitchell, who explained, "Needlepoint makes you relax when you have all the time in the world, but when you have to hurry, it makes you nervous." She does hope to find time again in the future, "if my eyes hold out," she says laughingly.

Many of the Cabinet wives, however, found needlepoint a pleasant addition to their current duties. Although there were no formal attempts at communal efforts or "sewing bees," Martha Mitchell recalls, "I did see some of them working at our meetings. You know, the Cabinet *wives* are always having meetings, too. There are parties to plan, decisions to make." Mrs. William Rogers, wife of the Secretary of State, was so enthusiastic about the project that after finishing her seal for Blair House, she asked for a duplicate to make as a personal gift for her husband. She also "ghosted" a seal for another Cabinet wife but diplomatically kept the name top secret.

All handiwork was turned in at a tea hosted by Mrs. Mitchell and Mrs. Emil Mosbacher, Jr., chairman of Blair House Fine Arts Committee and the wife of the Chief of Protocol. A talented needlewoman herself, Mrs. Mosbacher awarded each guest the "Order of the Lost Scissors," a brightly striped ribbon tied to a pair of scissors at one end and a pin cushion at the other.

Mrs. Spiro Agnew and Mrs. Richard M. Nixon, with their husbands' seals of office, two of the official seals stitched for Blair House by the U.S. Cabinet wives. Photo courtesy the Washington Star.

Now handsomely mounted in traditional black frames, the fourteen seals march in strict protocol—Mrs. Nixon's first, the others in proper order—up the stairway walls leading to Blair House's Head of State suite, a permanent reminder of President Nixon's original Cabinet members and their wives.

Favorite needlepoint: Fourteen seals of office of the Cabinet members, President, and Vice President. The circular seals are ten inches in diameter, the overall pictures thirteen by fifteen inches.

Design: Rosetta Larsen under the supervision of Elizabeth Draper, Blair House Interior designer

Canvas: No. 18 mono

Stitches: Basketweave for the background; continental for the seals

Amy Vanderbilt

"Is it rude to needlepoint after dinner when we have guests?"

"Should I take needlework with me to meetings?"

Concern with the etiquette of stitchery is often reflected among the thousands of inquiries received by Amy Vanderbilt, the well-known arbiter of good manners. The questions could not be directed toward a more sympathetic person, for Miss Vanderbilt is herself a needlepoint enthusiast who uses every appropriate moment to stitch. Her responses show the same combination of common sense and kindness evident in her popular books and column in *Ladies' Home Journal*.

"I see no objection whatever to women needlepointing after dinner in a social setting. It's very pleasant among friends. But I don't approve at all of taking needlework to meetings or concerts," she says emphatically. "When I was a lecturer, I was always distracted by women doing needlework. You see the tops of their heads from the lecture stand and think they couldn't possibly be listening." On the other hand, a lot depends upon the kind of meeting one is attending. "I took nee-

141

dlepoint to my Weight Watcher's group," Miss Vanderbilt reports, "and the leader said, 'That's a much better idea for your hands than using them to put food in your mouth.' "

Generally, Miss Vanderbilt endorses a home setting for needlepoint, particularly with one's family. "My husband enjoys watching me," she says with an obvious concern for pleasing him. "I think it gives most husbands a sense of being taken care of—the domesticity of it." One of the few public places she considers appropriate for stitchery is an airplane. "I often needlepoint on planes," she says, adding, "incidentally, that's a very nice way to meet people because they are interested in what you're doing and will always talk to you."

Miss Vanderbilt has enjoyed doing needlepoint for some years, all the more so since she was once awkward at manual work, having been a natural leftie forced into right handedness. Her first effort was a child's quick point kit project, depicting three choir boys in front of a stained-glass window, bought in preparation for a hospital stay. "During the long, dark night before the operation I started it, and when I found I was still alive the next day, I finished it before I came home." She gave it to a friend, then made a duplicate for another admiring friend.

A great deal of Miss Vanderbilt's needlepoint has been given away to friends and family. In addition, she stockpiles a variety of needlepoint kits for birthday presents or hostess gifts. "I often give little girls coasters to make—to get them started stitching," she says.

Despite her generosity with needlepoint, her New York town house still shows ample evidence of her enthusiasm. In her efficient book-lined office, current work in progress is kept near her desk where she takes advantage of free moments. On

Amy Vanderbilt's sentimental favorites are a pair of pillows with Danish toy soldiers that she made for her sons many years ago.

142

a lower floor, in a comfortable red-walled library overlooking a city garden, a pair of quickpoint daisy pillows are settled on a Victorian sofa. "They were inspired by our country place, Daisyfields, a name we also use for our family corporation," she explains. Her daughter-in-law admired them, so Miss Vanderbilt has made one for her. In another corner of the room, a suede-backed pillow faced with a needlepoint owl nestles in her husband's commodious Eames chair.

Obviously, her preference is for pillows. "I like to make them," she admits. "I like to be practical. I don't really enjoy needlepoint hangings or plaques. Of course, I'd love to make my husband a hunting vest," she confides, "but I'll never be that good. I like working on large-mesh canvas when I want quick results; then I can make a pillow for a friend or the children very fast. Other pieces slow me down discouragingly. I have several such in progress—lengthy progress."

Her favorite pieces of needlepoint are a pair of pillows on large-mesh canvas—two brightly stitched Danish toy soldiers made for her sons when they were young. Now showing the signs of wear that small boys sometimes inflict on the things they love, the pillows still rest on wicker rockers in the boys' old rooms. Miss Vanderbilt reminisces fondly, "My boys know Denmark well. They loved the Tivoli Gardens and often played with Danish wooden soldiers. So when I saw the canvases at a needlepoint shop, I wanted to stitch them."

The children are all grown now, one in the navy, another at college, and the eldest, a young publisher. Had she taught them to needlepoint? "No," she replies, "but I found the oldest a wife who can."

Favorite needlepoint: Wooden soldier pillows

Design: Alice Maynard, Inc., New York, in scarlet, yellow, beige, and black

Canvas: No. 5 penelope

Stitch: Continental

Betty White

In the company of one of her poodles, Betty White works on two long wall panels based on the blue and green marshflower print of her bedroom wallpaper.

At work or at play, Betty White is usually surrounded by animals, which suits her fine. As writer, producer, and star of "The Pet Set," she interviews celebrities (and their pets) on a half-hour weekly television show. Her own three dogs, two poodles and a "foundling would-be German shepherd retriever type," stay close by her side at home.

Small wonder, then, that Betty's favorite needlepoint comes from the animal kingdom. "I am especially fond of two framed wall hangings—a blue and gold macaw and a Mexican double yellow-headed parrot," she says exuberantly. She bought the painted canvases for both birds at needlepoint shops. "They were pretty good reproductions," she said, "but if you're a bird nut as I am, you see little things to change, so I ad-libbed around the faces and shading to make them as authentic as possible."

The parrot canvas measures eighteen by twenty inches, and the macaw is about an inch smaller. They are both stitched almost exclusively in basketweave, "except for minute detail," explains Betty, "and then it's every man for himself. They took about three months to stitch, and I generally worked on them before dinner when my husband [television personality Allen Ludden] and I have our 'happy hour' and catch up on the day."

The birds hang in the Ludden den framed as a pair but not identically. Pressed to pick her favorite between them, Betty reluctantly chose the parrot. "I used to have a similar parrot," she explains, "but I've always wanted a macaw."

Combining her two passions—animals and needlepoint—goes back to Betty's childhood, when she first became interested in stitchery. "When I was fourteen I was given figurines of the Gingham Dog and the Calico Cat, a favorite poem of mine. I drew them on graph paper, then counted the stitches on canvas. They weren't masterpieces," she acknowledges, "but they were pretty good for a fourteen-year-old's first try. I still have them hanging in our upstairs hall over the figurines."

Betty frequently sees ideas for needlepoint in all kinds of unexpected places. For one pillow she copied a favorite summer dress print by tracing the wildflower design on paper, then transferring it to canvas herself. "I thought I had used a waterproof marker," she reports, "but after the pillow was blocked, I found the marker had run and had created an amazing effect. It looked as if I had the talent and the imagination to make a line of pale blue shading on just one side of all the flowers. It's the most gorgeous effect—like a shadow print! Isn't that a beautiful lagniappe?" Her current project was inspired by her bedroom wallpaper, a blue and green marshflower print that she has traced onto two long panels planned to hang on a paneled bedroom wall.

Betty White, a "bird nut," stitched this blue and gold macaw (left). She traced the design of a favorite dress print and transferred it to canvas for the gay floral pillow (right).

Needlepoint abounds in the Ludden's Los Angeles home. Nine songbirds perch on a bellpull, and flower pillows and wall hangings dot the rooms, although Betty's needlepoint is just as likely to be given away as it is to find a place in her home. "I've done several pillows and a couple of framed pieces for gifts," she says. "I think it's a nice, personal kind of present, and I usually like to give animals or birds." She has also been the recipient. "Beverly Garland had been on my show when we did a sequence with a giraffe," she recalls. "For my birthday she sent me an adorable giraffe with the yarn to stitch it. I named him George, and I've just finished him."

"Needlepoint is great relaxation, and constantly fascinating to me," Betty continues. "And Allen takes such an interest that it makes it fun. I've always loved any kind of handwork.

Betty White is especially fond of this Mexican double yellow-headed parrot.

My fingers itch. And your mind can work while your hands are busy. I'm such an addict," she admits, "that I stay about three projects ahead at all times."

What's next on her agenda? "I'm dying to try some different stitches, and perhaps frame them with a border stitch. Or make a pattern in bas relief." And, never tiring of combining her love of animals with stitchery, she adds, "I've even been toying with the idea of doing my dogs in needlepoint."

Favorite needlepoint: Mexican double yellow-headed parrot, eighteen by twenty inches

Design: By Jebba, Inc., Los Angeles, California, with additions by Miss White; in yellow, shades of greens, rust, and blues on a pale background

Canvas: No. 14 mono

Stitch: Basketweave

Needlepoint Refresher

STITCHES

Along with their favorite needlepoint projects, the celebrities included in this book often have favorite needlepoint stitches. As a reminder of how to do the various stitches used, here are brief instructions:

Continental, or Tent, Stitch

A popular stitch for use on either mono or penelope canvas, the continental can be used for outlining shapes, filling in details, and covering large background areas. It provides a well-padded backing for projects requiring durability but tends to distort the canvas.

Work the continental from the right side of the row to the left, then turn the canvas upside down to work the return row from right to left again (see Fig. 1). To outline shapes, make the same stitches on a row from top to bottom; change direction

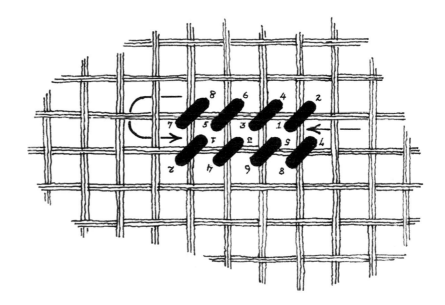

Figure 1.

simply by turning the canvas upside down. Keep your stitches loose to minimize distortion of the canvas.

To see the continental stitch in a finished piece, turn to photographs of the favorite needlepoint of Claire Bloom, Rocky Converse, Kathryn Crosby, Ann B. Davis, Julie Eisenhower, Hermione Gingold, Rosey Grier, Abbe Lane, Roberta Peters, U.S. Cabinet wives, and Amy Vanderbilt.

Half Cross Stitch The half cross closely resembles the continental on the front of a canvas, but it can only be worked on penelope and provides very little padding on the back. Use it for outlining shapes, filling in details, and covering large areas of background. Like the continental, it tends to distort the canvas.

Work the half cross from the left side of the row to the

153

right, then turn the canvas upside down so you can also work the return row from left to right (see Fig. 2). You can outline shapes by stitching rows from top to bottom and then changing direction by simply turning the canvas upside down. Loose stitches will keep distortion to a minimum.

Figure 2.

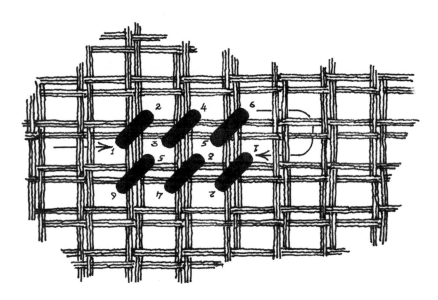

  To see the half cross stitch, turn to the photograph of the favorite needlepoint piece of Janet Leigh.

Quick Point Stitch This hybrid stitch, a combination of continental and half cross, eliminates the necessity of turning the canvas upside down after each row. It can only be done on penelope canvas and is particularly popular on a large, No. 5 mesh on which it works up quickly. It has a fair amount of padding but distorts the canvas.

154

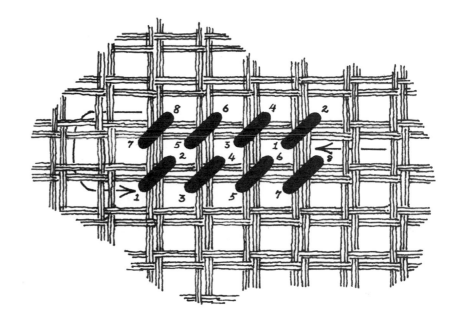

Figure 3.

To do quick point, work one row in continental from right to left, then work the next row in half cross, stitching from left to right (see Fig. 3).

To see what finished quick point looks like, turn to the photograph of Meredith MacRae's pillow.

Basketweave Stitch

Basketweave looks very much like continental and half cross from the front but does not distort the canvas as they do. It is worked on either penelope or mono and has a closely woven padding, which is particularly useful for heavy-wear articles such as upholstery and rugs. It is used primarily to fill in solid areas or background. Because it is difficult to maintain in sections with small shapes or detailed designs, it is sometimes used in conjunction with the continental or half cross.

Start the basketweave stitch at the top right corner of your

155

canvas (the lower left, if you're left handed). Work in diagonal rows, first going down the canvas from left to right, then up the canvas from right to left (see Fig. 4). There is no need to turn the canvas upside down. Although the basketweave stitch might look difficult at first glance, there is a simple and logical rhythm to the sequence of stitches.

For examples of finished basketweave, see the photographs of the favorite needlepoint projects of Kathryn Crosby, Ann B. Davis, Joan Fontaine, Betty Furness, Princess Grace, Muriel Humphrey, Maria Cooper Janis, Melanie Kahane, Abbe Lane, Clare Boothe Luce, Russell Lynes, Dina Merrill, Mary Tyler Moore, Mr. and Mrs. Louis Nizer, Mollie Parnis, Lyn Revson, Dorothy Rodgers, Aline Saarinen, U.S. Cabinet wives, and Betty White.

Figure 4.

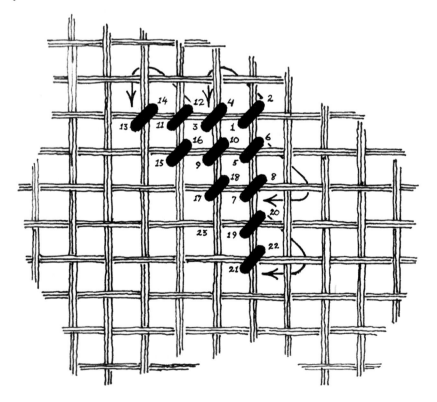

Mosaic Stitch   Suitable for both mono and penelope canvas, the mosaic makes a boxlike pattern that is particularly attractive as a background for a central figure. The stitch is quick to work and gives a firm padding, but tends to distort the canvas.

Work the stitch from the right side of the canvas to the left, then turn the canvas upside down so that you still stitch the return row from right to left (see Fig. 5).

Figure 5.

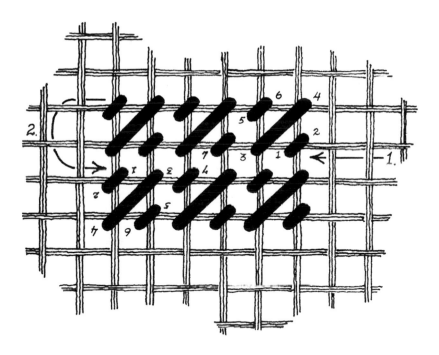

For an example of the mosaic stitch framing a central figure, see the photograph of Dorothy Rodgers' favorite needlepoint pillow.

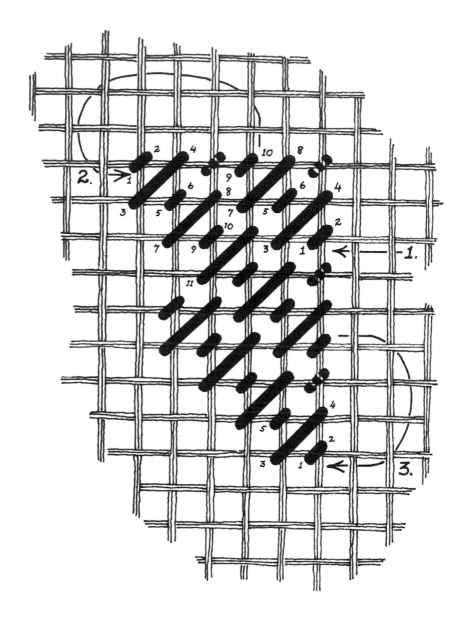

Figure 6.

Diagonal Mosaic Stitch　　When the mosaic stitch is worked on the diagonal on either mono or penelope canvas, its boxlike pattern is transformed into diagonal stripes that make an attractive background.

158

Make your rows of stitches diagonally, first going up the canvas from right to left, then down from left to right (see Fig. 6) without turning the canvas upside down. Around the edges where you can't complete an entire stitch, fill in with individual continental stitches as needed (broken lines in Fig. 6).

To see how the diagonal mosaic is used to frame sections of a rug, see the photograph of Muriel Humphrey's favorite needlepoint.

Brick Stitch

The bricklike pattern of this stitch is most successful on mono canvas. A particularly useful stitch, it works up quickly, is durable, won't distort the canvas, and gives an attractive texture to the background of your piece.

Work your rows back and forth without turning the canvas around (see Fig. 7). For adequate coverage you may need

Figure 7.

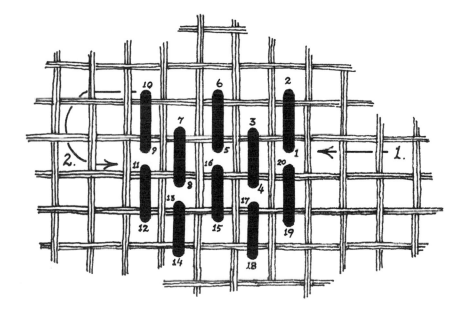

159

one more strand of yarn than you are using for other slanting stitches on the same canvas. Keep wool untwisted and flat for neat, full stitches.

You can see a brick stitch background in Melanie Kahane's bench cushion.

Upright Cross Stitch   This durable stitch forms an interesting pebbled texture that is effective for background or pattern details. It can be used on either mono or penelope canvas and works up speedily. Stitch from left to right (see Fig. 8), then, without turning canvas, return from right to left. The top stitches must all be taken in the same direction.

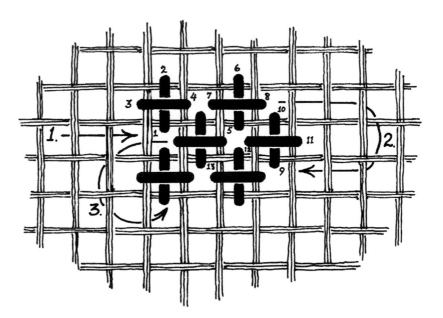

Figure 8.

To see the upright cross stitch in use, turn to the illustration of Melanie Kahane's bench cushion.

Figure 9.

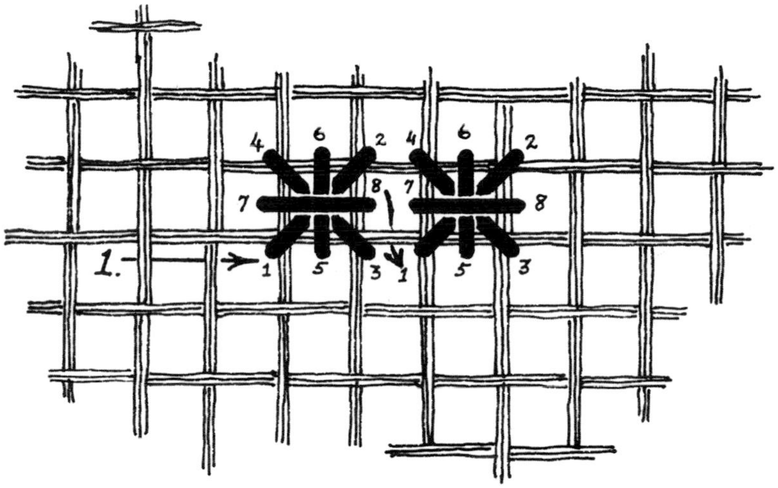

Smyrna Cross Stitch	This decorative stitch, which can be used on mono or penelope canvas, adds texture to a design.

The stitch is made over two horizontal and two vertical canvas threads (see Fig. 9). When making more than one Smyrna cross, be sure that the strokes in each stitch are made in the same order and especially that the top strokes all point in the same direction.

This stitch is used effectively in the border of Melanie Kahane's turtle bench cushion.

Double Leviathan Stitch	The double leviathan, a bumpy, popcornlike stitch, is an enlarged version of the Smyrna cross and is used for even more pronounced textural effect. Suitable for mono or penelope canvas, it makes striking accents.

This stitch is made over four horizontal and four vertical

161

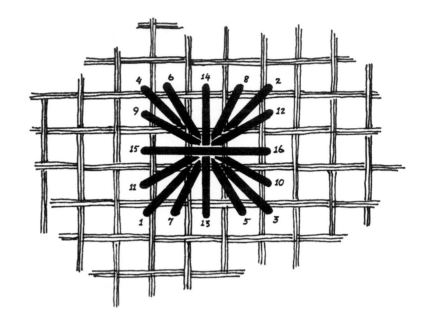

Figure 10.

canvas threads (see Fig. 10). When making more than one, be sure that the strokes in each stitch are made in the same sequence and that the top strokes all point in the same direction.

The double leviathan forms the bumps on the turtle shell in Melanie Kahane's bench cushion.

Bargello

Bargello is not one single stitch, but is really a series of vertical stitches made in one of many patterns. It can be a long, continuous line, moving up and down at preset intervals, with the changes in those intervals determining the pattern of the line. Or the sequence of vertical stitches can be rounded or shaped so as to form self-enclosed patterns that look like diamonds, hearts, scallops, and other shapes. The constant in bargello is that the stitches are made vertically, covering two to six threads

—but most usually covering four—with the steps between each stitch ranging from one to four, but usually changing at two. You can change the pattern by altering either the number of threads each vertical stitch covers or the step sequence.

The most familiar bargello pattern is a continuous line with sharp zigs and zags, sometimes known as the Florentine or flame stitch, after the flamelike pattern it produces. A simple version is illustrated in Figure 11. Center the pattern on your canvas and then work one "tracking row," which will serve as your guide for all subsequent rows. You can make the stitches in any direction: to the left, the right, up, or down. To be sure your yarn covers the canvas properly when making these verti-

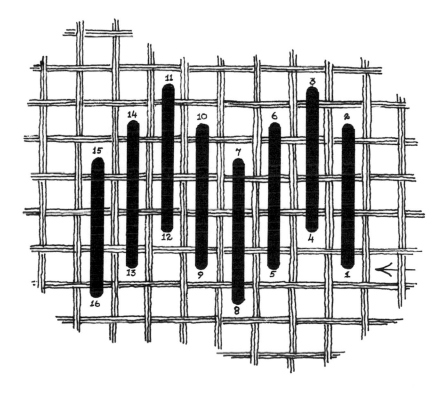

Figure 11.

cal stitches, keep your wool flat and add an extra strand if necessary.

Bargello is often worked in graded tones of the same color, but you can use many different color combinations, even working the same pattern in different combinations for varied effects. To see a variety of bargello patterns, including one worked in different color schemes, turn to the pictures of Betty Furness's bargello pillows and canvases.

PREPARING THE CANVAS

Cut your canvas two inches larger than your design on all sides. (This is in addition to any seam allowance you may have included.) The excess canvas is needed for later blocking. To protect the cut edges of the canvas from raveling, bind them with one-inch masking tape.

If you plan to upholster furniture with needlepoint, outline the area to be covered on a piece of brown paper, adding a one-inch seam allowance on all sides, plus any depth measurement. Leave the canvas square or rectangular, even if the design you have drawn on it is circular, oval, or another irregular shape.

PUTTING YOUR DESIGN ON CANVAS

To transfer a design to canvas, lay the prepared canvas on a table. Over it, center the design face down and tape the corners of the design to the back of the canvas. Then turn it over. If the outline of your design is dark enough, you can place the canvas on a white surface (piece of paper, tabletop, or even a sheet) and see the design clearly enough to trace onto the canvas. If the design is not well outlined, you will need to place the canvas on a glass tabletop and underlight it with a lamp in order to see through it for tracing. If you don't have a glass table, use a large windowpane where the sun can backlight your design.

Now transfer your design to the canvas, using a completely indelible felt marker. Choose a marker in a neutral color, rather than a dark one, unless your yarns are dark; otherwise, your tracing may show through light-colored wools.

After outlining your design on canvas, you can indicate color on your design *paper* or on the canvas itself. If done on the paper, just crayon or write the colors and carry the paper with you as your guide. If done on the canvas, indicate color in different design areas with indelible markers or paint the entire canvas with acrylic paints. When working with acrylics, thin them with water only until the paint flows freely but doesn't saturate the canvas.

If your design is not exactly the right size for your needlepoint project—which would be the case, for example, if you took it from a large poster or from the smaller pages of a book —it can be reduced or enlarged photostatically. Simply take the original design to a photoenlarger, give him the finished dimensions, and ask for the positive (he will normally only furnish a negative). If you are deriving your design from an object you can't readily take to a photoenlarger—drapery fabric or a china plate are common examples—you can trace the design and have the tracing photostatically enlarged or reduced.

To transfer the photostat to canvas, follow the procedures described above and treat the photostat like the design.

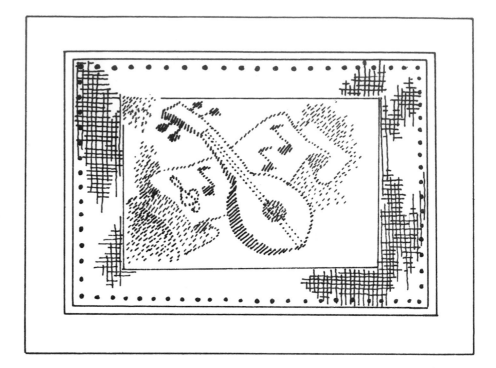

Figure 12.

BLOCKING

Blocking gives a professional look to your work and is usually required to correct distortion in the canvas resulting from uneven stitching.

Tack a sheet of brown paper to a piece of plywood large enough to accommodate your needlepoint. Then place your stitchery face down on the paper, and tack the upper left and upper right corners of the unworked canvas border with nonrusting pins or tacks. Lightly wet the back of the needlepoint, either by steaming it with an iron held a few inches above the surface, or by sponging or spraying the back with water. The canvas will now be flexible enough for you to pull the other two corners into shape and tack them securely. Tack all four sides at one-inch intervals about an inch out from the finished stitching (never through it), pulling and tugging as needed to correct any distortion (see Fig. 12). A badly misshaped canvas may have to be steamed or sponged twice during blocking. After tacking, let the canvas dry thoroughly (perhaps two days).